D0490074

GOING

Manchester City's PETER REID huffs and puffs as he beats off the challenge of CLAYTON BLACKMORE (Manchester United).

Price £3.75

The Topical
FOOTBALL

Contents

imes BOOK

FOUR MONTHS THAT SHOOK THE KOP!

OUT — Kenny Dalglish

SEASON 1990-91 was one of the most traumatic in the history of Liverpool Football Club. Blow after blow was handed out to the Merseyside team during a campaign filled with set-backs and disappointments. Here are the major incidents in that crushing four-month period from which the team could not recover.

JANUARY 5

An FA Cup third round tie versus Blackburn. Liverpool escape being dumped by the narrowest of margins. Trailing 1-0 at Ewood Park until the 89th minute, Liverpool are saved when Rovers' defender Mark Atkins puts the ball into his own net. Liverpool's Glenn Hysen and Blackburn's Kevin Moran both get their marching orders in an ill-tempered game.

JANUARY 8

The FA Cup third round replay versus Blackburn. Ray Houghton is put out of action for over a month after picking up a bad thigh injury. The Irishman had scored his 7th goal of the season during the match. Steve McMahon is ordered off for persistent fouling. The only bright spot — Liverpool win through to the next round. Kenny Dalglish says, "This club has had the best disciplinary record for the past three years. We've won the Fair Play trophy each time. But in the past two games we have had more players sent off than in the previous three years. We need to take a long, hard look at the system."

FEBRUARY 9

Ronnie Whelan is out for the rest of the season after breaking his fibula during the 3-1 League win over Everton.
Whelan says afterwards, "There is no way I've given up hope of playing again this season."
But unfortunately for Ronnie and Liverpool he did not take any further part in the season's proceedings.

FEBRUARY 17

The FA Cup fifth round game versus Everton is drawn but it brings yet another injury blow. Influential midfielder Steve McMahon is carried off after tackling Everton's John Ebbrell. The injury turns out to be damaged knee ligaments, which put McMahon out for the rest of the season.

FEBRUARY 20

The FA Cup fifth round replay versus Everton. One of the greatest derby games ever seen. The Reds go ahead FOUR times during the match, but resilient Everton fight back each time. Supersub Tony Cottee scores twice after coming on in the 86th minute, Graeme Sharp gets the other two. Rush, Barnes and Beardsley (2) score for Liverpool. Manager Kenny Dalglish later blasts: "We gave it away."

FEBRUARY 22

Liverpool are hit with their biggest bombshell since being ordered out of Europe in 1985. Kenny Dalglish resigns as manager! The news comes at a bad time for the club as Arsenal breathe down their necks in the championship race.
At the press conference to announce his decision, Kenny tells a shocked audience, "The biggest problem was the pressure I was putting myself under because of my desire to be successful. It would have been wrong to mislead people that everything was fine with me."

FEBRUARY 27

The FA Cup fifth round second replay versus Everton. Liverpool's season goes from bad to worse. Their dreams of the double are ruined when Everton's Dave Watson scores the only goal of the game.
Caretaker-manager Ronnie Moran insists he is "still smiling."

MARCH 1

Alan Hansen adds to Liverpool's woe as he quits the game after eight Championship winners' medals and 620 games for the club. Ruling himself out as a contender for the manager's job, Hansen says, "I had a final scan on my injured right knee and the specialist advised me to pack it in. My decision has absolutely nothing to do with Kenny Dalglish. I made up my mind to retire three weeks ago."

APRIL 2

Liverpool virtually hand the title to Arsenal as they go down 1-0 to Southampton. It isn't turning out to be Liverpool's season. The man who scores the goal against them is one they tried so hard to sign last season — Matthew Le Tissier.

APRIL 16

A shock on a par with Dalglish's resignation is the appointment of new Anfield boss Graeme Souness. Souness had previously ruled himself out of the running until doing a U-turn and moving to Merseyside.
Souness says on his arrival, "My first priorty is to see if Liverpool can win the championship. We are points adrift but nothing is impossible in football. I have seen Liverpool a few times this season and in my opinion they are still the best club side in Britain, maybe in Europe and maybe the world."

MAY 6

Arsenal take the title as Liverpool go down 2-1 to Nottingham Forest. The man who scores the winning goal is Forest winger Ian Woan — a lifelong Liverpool fan.
Graeme Souness, 'celebrating' his 38th birthday, declares, "I would say that Liverpool have lost it more than Arsenal have won it. I want to know how much it is hurting the players. Any team of mine should be hurting badly."
Season 1990-91 was one Liverpool will want to forget. Now Graeme Souness faces the challenge of putting them back on top.

IN — Graeme Souness

GARY LINEKER *Tottenham Hotspur*

PAUL BEESLEY *Sheffield Utd.*

I'M GLAD THE BOSS

I'M still amazed at the way last season ended for me — with international recognition and a place in the England senior squad. Now I want to make the most of my new confidence, and establish a permanent place. I've set my sights on being in the England squad for the European Championship Finals in Sweden next summer — if we qualify.

I've got to admit that my selection came as just as big a surprise to me as it did to most other people. But I just tried to grab the chance when it arrived.

Last season was a big disappointment for me at club level. My form was very patchy. International football wasn't really in my thoughts, when, out of the blue, I was called up for the game in Turkey.

Looking back I can name the turning point — the day I was dropped by Chelsea! There can't be many players who can say they owe their first international cap to being dropped from their club team.

But being left out for a few games by the manager certainly did me a favour. It really livened me up. I wasn't happy at the time, but I soon realised the boss was right. He did it to a few of us at Chelsea. Kerry Dixon was also left out, and came back really 'flying'.

I knew I had not been playing my best, and the manager told me I had to liven up. I did so, and the result was my England selection.

People expected a lot of both myself and Chelsea at the start of last season. Perhaps there was too much pressure on me. When you move for a big fee, as I did when joining Chelsea from Wimbledon, everybody expects a lot. But it takes time to settle into a new team.

DENNIS WISE

DROPPED ME!

Chelsea use a different type of game to Wimbledon. It was a question of getting used to a new style of play and new team-mates.

It didn't help being sent off early in the season, against Crystal Palace. But I don't blame that incident for my patchy form. The sending-off didn't affect me. I've always been a player who gets involved in tackling, and winning the ball, but it was a scuffle off the ball that I was sent off for. I never worried about getting into trouble again for making tackles.

I haven't had to change my game at all. I think Graham Taylor wanted me to play exactly the same way for England as I did at my best for Wimbledon — working hard to win the ball, and then delivering good crosses.

Wingers are there to get crosses in, to create chances — and perhaps score goals. Getting a goal on my England debut against Turkey — even one I didn't see go in the net — was an added thrill for me.

I saw Gary Pallister's header across goal looping towards me at the far post, and I just lunged at the ball. I didn't see what happened to it, but I suddenly realised the ball was in the net. What a great feeling!

The way the season ended justified my leaving Wimbledon. I joined Chelsea because they are a bigger club. I thought it would give me a better chance of winning international selection.

As it happens, Graham Taylor has shown he doesn't worry about what club you play for. Last season he picked three Wimbledon players for the England B team, and seems prepared to have a look at anyone.

There was quite a fuss when I was picked for the squad, while Chris Waddle was left out. But that didn't concern me. It wasn't my problem. Why should I worry about anyone else? Every player has his ups and downs, and you just have to get on with it.

It was a big boost to my confidence to get picked, and that's all I'm worried about. I feel my type of game is right for Graham Taylor's method. He likes to have a big man up front, very much the way teams like Arsenal, Wimbledon and Palace play. I feel I can supply an accurate service for the target man.

It's ironic that Mr Taylor's right-hand man is Lawrie McMenemy — the man who gave me a free transfer from Southampton when I was a youngster. By coincidence, I signed for Chelsea the week after Andy Townsend, who was also at the Dell with me.

KERRY DIXON

People thought we were the last pieces in the jig-saw at Stamford Bridge and that Chelsea would immediately challenge for the title and all the cups. But football is not like that.

It takes time for a team to settle together. This season we have a much better chance of success. We will be disappointed if things don't go well.

Our best performances last season were all against the better teams, which shows our potential. We were the only side to beat Arsenal in the League; and we ended Liverpool's chances of the title by beating them 4-2.

Perhaps our best performance was beating Spurs in the Rumbelows Cup, at White Hart Lane. We played really well to win 3-0. That result put us into the semi-finals, and we thought it could be our year. But we failed against Sheffield Wednesday both at home and away. That was our biggest disappointment of the season.

I was beginning to dream of playing in a Wembley final again, reviving memories of Wimbledon's FA Cup win over Liverpool. Only my England debut in Turkey rivals that as the highlight in my career.

I certainly hope to be going back to Wembley with Chelsea in the next year or two.

MICKY GYNN *Coventry*

IT HAPPENED LAST SEASON!

Test your memory about the events of 1990-91

STUART PEARCE
(Nottingham Forest)
— see question 4.

1. One English First Division match ended in a 7-1 victory to the visiting team. Can you name the two sides involved?

2. Manchester United used a total of four goalkeepers throughout the campaign. How many can you remember?

3. Queen's Park Rangers had to wait until October before their new World Cup goalkeeper was able to join them. Can you name him and the country he represented in the World Cup Finals in Italy?

4. Stuart Pearce stopped taking Nottingham Forest's penalties after his miss from the spot in England's World Cup semi-final shoot-out defeat by West Germany. Who took over his City Ground penalty duties?

5. Who scored both Rangers' goals in their Scottish Premier Division Championship decider against Aberdeen?

6. Who scored the first goal for an English club in Europe after the lifting of the ban imposed following the Heysel Stadium disaster?

7. Who was he playing for and can you recall the name and nationality of the opposition?

8. Everton manager Howard Kendall went a long way in his search for players, even into Eastern Europe. Which Polish international did he snap up for £450,000 from Gornik Zabrze?

9. Who won the Scottish Centenary Cup competition and who were the beaten finalists?

10. Arsenal's defence was the most miserly in the Football League. How many goals did Tony Adams, David Seaman and company concede?

11. Who scored a goal and saved a penalty in the same League game?

12. Who scored on his debut for England and which other player made his international debut during the same match?

13. Who won the Superskills award in the Scottish League?

14. Can you name the four teams who won automatic promotion from the Fourth Division?

15. What was unusual about the three teams promoted automatically from Division Three?

16. A Scot was voted Footballer of the Year at the age of 34. Name and club, please.

17. A tiny footballing nation scored one of the game's most outstanding victories ever. The 1-0 win came against Austria in the European Championships. Who were the giant killers?

18. Scotland also tackled a trip into the unknown when they faced another country new to the international soccer scene. This country is actually a part of northern Italy. What is it called?

19. Kenny Dalglish had a final fling in the transfer market before his shock resignation from Liverpool. He signed three big-money players in quick succession. Can you name them, their fees and their former clubs?

20. A new chairman was elected to the Professional Footballers' Association. He once won a Championship medal at Highbury but was transferred north for £350,000 last term. Name and current club, please.

21. Four Scottish clubs were promoted, two from the First and two from the Second Division. How many can you name?

ANSWERS ON PAGE 124

LIFTING the FA Cup at Wembley last May was a magical moment but the memories I will treasure most are of the supporters who cheered us next day. Thousands of ordinary people from young babies to grandmothers came to welcome us.

Four years before, it was the fans turning out to greet us in Tottenham, although we'd lost the FA Cup Final to Coventry City, who really made up for our own disappointment.

To be back last season with the FA Cup, after having had so many problems during the year, made everything worthwhile.

Against Coventry, the winning goal came when I deflected a shot into our goal past Ray Clemence. Headlines in the papers said 'Mabbutt's error costs Spurs the Cup'.

I was really upset. It was the worst moment of my playing career. But riding on the open-topped bus around

CUPHOLDER
GARY LINEKER

Tottenham, I could see lots of banners saying 'We don't blame you, Gary'. That really cheered me up.

At the end of the day, supporters are what football is all about. If there were no football fans, there would be no professional football. In many ways supporters are more important than players.

The reaction of the fans in 1987 played a big part in my signing a new contract that year to stay at White Hart Lane. It was not an easy decision, because Liverpool wanted me, and when you are ambitious you want to play for the best team.

But Spurs had reached the FA Cup Final, the Littlewoods Cup semi-final, and finished third in the First Division. I really felt we were ready to emulate Liverpool — and we had those superb supporters.

I signed a new five-year contract that summer, turning down the approaches from Liverpool. With the squad, and the formula developed by manager David Pleat, I thought we were ready to win some trophies.

But within three months the manager had gone, and almost half of that squad had moved on. It has been a struggle ever since.

Winning the Cup finally made up for many of the disappointments. It is just unfortunate there have been so many financial problems at White Hart Lane, taking the shine off the Wembley success.

I think it said everything about the professionalism of the players at Tottenham that we were able to to get to Wembley at all.

Right from the start of the competition there had been increasingly worrying stories about the club's debts.

Manager Terry Venables tried to shield the players from the boardroom troubles. But players always want to know what's going on — it's only natural. It is a worry for players when it is their future that's involved.

As skipper I found myself as the go-between. The manager kept me informed on developments, and I passed it on to the other players.

It was very difficult. Every time you picked up a paper, you wondered what next you were going to read about the club.

The on-off, on-off transfer saga of Paul Gascoigne was particularly unsettling for everyone. However, we are all professionals, and whatever is happening off the field, we have to put it to the back of our minds, and get on with the job.

JUST *Magic!*

That's the verdict of Spurs' GARY MABBUTT on his side's triumph at Wembley.

Gazza's injury at Wembley was tragic for him, especially after he did so much to get us to the final. He was our inspiration.

Before the Rugby League Challenge Cup Final, I heard the Wigan manager talking about the importance to them of Ellery Hanley. He was prepared to play Hanley at Wembley even if he were only 20 per cent fit, because of his psychological effect on the other players.

Paul Gascoigne was like that for Spurs last season. He lifted the team just by being out there on the pitch.

Long before the final — and his injury — I was resigned to him leaving Spurs for Italy. It was disappointing, but nobody could deny him the chance to make his fortune.

I believe he has the ability to make himself one of the best players ever produced in England. Perhaps the greatest of all. He is so skilled and strong.

Gazza's injury at Wembley was the result of over-enthusiasm. But that exuberance and enthusiasm is part of his game. If you took it away, he wouldn't be the same player. He just needs to learn how to control it.

Gazza is learning all the time, but he still needs players around him to calm him down and bring him back to earth. He has grown up a lot in the last year — and the Cup Final experience, as long

as he recovers fully, will be another valuable lesson.

The World Cup did him a lot of good, on and off the field. He matured a great deal in those few weeks. He was so naive and young for his age when he first joined Spurs, it was unbelievable.

But the great thing is, there's not an ounce of malice in him. He's popular with everybody at White Hart Lane.

Last season I tried to stay as close as possible to Gazza on the field if things were threatening to boil over. I would just have a quiet word to cool him down.

Referees often had a chat with me if Gazza was getting close to the mark, and I would tell him to calm down. I had to try to protect him, he was so important to the team.

When he was carried off in the final, with Spurs a goal down, we just had to roll up our sleeves and win it without him. It was great to come back like that — but we'd rather have done it with Gazza.

Wembley wasn't the only highlight for me towards the end of last season. I also regained a place in the England senior squad for the European Championship match in Turkey.

It was due to injuries to other players — but it was still nice to travel with England again, after a gap of over three years. I certainly hope that won't be my last trip.

It was a disappointment for me to drop out of Bobby Robson's international squad, and miss the 1986 World Cup and the 1988 European finals. I felt I played pretty consistently for my club in that period.

I would never say that I should have been picked. But I believe I'm the type of player who would have benefitted the squad.

In my 13 senior internationals, I have started in five different positions. With that kind of experience, I think I could have been a useful squad member.

However, I'm still pleased to have got into 20 or 30 England squads, and won those 13 caps. I've always considered it an honour to get a call-up.

When I was left out, I never thought of it as being all over for me at international level. I've just done my best for my club, and hoped for another chance for England. I still do.

I'm proud of my record in representative games. Five times I have captained the England B team, and we won all five without conceding a goal.

Also, I have led the Football League team, captained the Under-21 side three times, and the England Youth team once.

It's a personal thing. It's always a thrill for me to lead out a team, at club or international level. Despite all the ups and downs, I have enjoyed captaining Spurs.

They have always been one of the biggest clubs. You expect a lot of publicity at a place like Tottenham. They are usually in the headlines.

Players are always coming and going. I've been 'sold' about five times myself, according to the newspapers! You get used to it and learn to take everything with a pinch of salt.

The problem last season was that most of the stories about Spurs' financial problems were true! It would have been better if they had been unfounded rumours.

However, you have to get over setbacks if you want to be successful. As a youngster I had to overcome the blow of discovering I was a diabetic.

At first I thought it meant the end of my football career. But I have learned how to cope, and doing that has helped me to deal with the other disappointments.

Winning the FA Cup last season was a great reward. I hope there will be others.

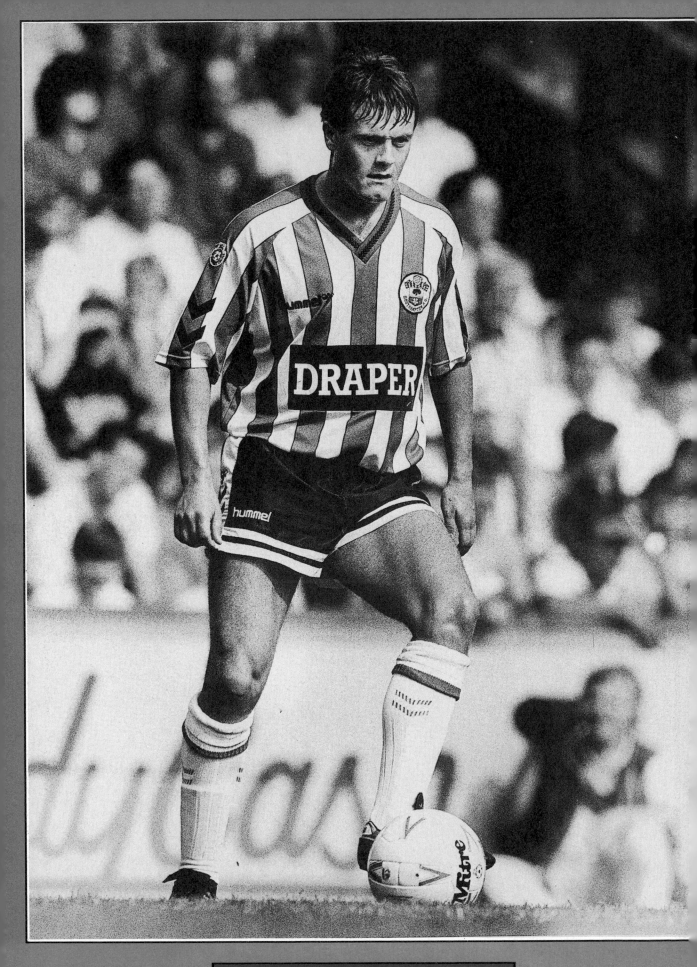

MICKY ADAMS *Southampton*

STUART McCALL
Everton

I AM beginning to wonder if I will ever get to Wembley with Norwich. Over the last few years we've been so close — only to let ourselves down on the big occasion.

In 1989, we travelled to Villa Park for an FA Cup semi-final against Everton. After a great season in the League we were confident we could beat the Merseyside team and take the club and our fans to their first-ever FA Cup Final.

There were over 46,000 fans in the ground that day and they created a great atmosphere. Unfortunately, that put the players under a lot of pressure and our performance suffered as a result.

Pat Nevin put Everton in front and after that we were chasing the game until the final whistle went. When it finally came, we felt terrible — we'd come so close to Wembley only to miss out at the final hurdle.

But our disappointment soon became irrelevant minutes later when we heard the full details of the terrible tragedy involving Liverpool fans at the other semi-final at Hillsborough. You had to forget about football at a time like that.

Even if we had beaten Everton that day at Villa Park it is highly unlikely that we would ever have played in the FA Cup Final. It was only because it was an all-Merseyside final that it eventually went ahead.

Our quest for a place at Wembley continued last season in the FA Cup and the Zenith Data Systems Cup. But it was all to fizzle out in the space of ten disappointing days.

We'd won our place in the FA Cup quarter-finals with a tremendous win over Manchester United, who up to then had swept everybody aside in an all-conquering cup season. The confidence of that Carrow Road victory set us up perfectly for another home tie in the quarter-finals against Nottingham Forest.

WE'LL BEAT THAT
Wembley Jinx!

That's the vow of Norwich City's MARK BOWEN

Earlier in the season at home we'd lost 6-2 to Brian Clough's team! This was the FA Cup, though, and we were ready for a taste of revenge. Unfortunately, it turned out to be a very disappointing game — particularly for us.

Just when we needed to be at our best, we froze. Yet again we let the big occasion get to us. It wasn't that we were short on possession, in fact we had the majority of the play, but we just couldn't hold our nerve in front of goal — and they could.

It was bitterly disappointing to have missed out in the FA Cup but at least we had another chance to make Wembley. That came in the Zenith Data Cup against Crystal Palace.

Earlier in the season, we probably didn't take that competition very seriously. The League, the FA Cup and the Rumbelows Cup all took priority. But when you are just one game away from Wembley, as we were against Palace, you start to realise the possible rewards of the competition.

Unfortunately, we were to waste yet another Wembley chance with a couple of poor performances over the two legs. I couldn't believe that we'd let

everybody down again.

Despite all the recent disappointments with Norwich, I do at least have one happy memory of Wembley even if it was a long time ago.

Back in 1979, I went there as a 15-year-old to play for Wales Schoolboys against England. That was quite a thrill in itself, but scoring the Welsh goal in a 1-1 draw gives me particularly strong reasons for remembering the game. Whatever else happens in my career, I'll always be able to say I scored at Wembley!

It was soon after that game that I started my apprenticeship at Tottenham Hotspur. They'd spotted me playing in the Neath area of Wales where I was brought up — a place better known for producing rugby players than footballers.

Indeed, like most Welsh boys, I was much more interested in rugby union than football. I used to play scrum-half for my school and dream of playing for Wales.

When I went along to watch my heroes playing in internationals at Cardiff Arms Park, I couldn't have guessed that I would play there one day myself — for the Welsh football team!

My ambition to follow in the footsteps of Gareth Edwards and other great scrum-halfs finally ended when I chose a career in football instead. You could make a living in football, but that was not really possible in rugby.

So, it was off to London to try my luck with Tottenham. I went to White Hart Lane as a midfielder but, by the time I left nine years later, most people thought of me as a left-back.

The strength of Tottenham at that time was also my biggest problem — the number of quality midfield players. In Glenn Hoddle, Ricky Villa and Ossie Ardiles they had three of the best in the world — not just in the country.

It was a great education for a young player like myself to train with the likes of Glenn and Ossie because you were

DAVE STRINGER

IAN CROOK

club, I even thought we were going to win the championship.

We had little indication of what an exciting campaign the 1988-89 season would be for us. Indeed, before the season started, things had been going very badly. Pre-season was a real disaster and we lost to everybody — mostly very lowly opposition. It looked like we were in for a real struggle. But when the season proper started, we were transformed. We won our first four games and seven of our first ten.

From the beginning of October until the end of December we were top of the table. We were playing good football and enjoying the pressure of being the League leaders.

It was in the second half of the season that the real questions would be asked of the team. Could we really keep it going and stay ahead of Arsenal and Liverpool who were snapping at our heels?

Unfortunately, I don't think we ever really believed that we could do it. Eventually that lack of confidence seeped through into our performances and game by game it all slipped away. The wheels finally came off when we were beaten 5-0 at Arsenal, who went on to win the title in a dramatic last game at Liverpool.

It was a big disappointment for everybody at Carrow Road to finish that season with nothing in the League or the Cup. But at least it did win us a bit more respect as a side, as well as bringing several players to the attention of other clubs.

For the next year or so I seemed to be a target for several clubs. One of the interested parties was Tottenham but I think they baulked at the idea of spending ten times what they'd sold me for in the first place!

There were apparently other clubs looking at me but nothing ever came of it all. In the end I settled for a new contract at Norwich.

Not that I was unhappy about staying in East Anglia — especially after I was made club captain last season. That was the icing on the cake as far as I was concerned.

I took over when Ian Butterworth, the skipper at the time, asked for a move himself. When the boss, Dave Stringer, looked around the dressing-room for a new man for the job, I was the one he picked.

I've always found that having a good old shout at the players around me works wonders for my concentration. It focuses my mind on the job I've got to do.

The boss obviously wanted somebody who wasn't afraid to open his mouth to keep all the others on their toes. I probably come out with just a lot of nonsense but I don't think that matters too much.

Now my ambition for this season has to be to lead Norwich to some success. It's about time we broke that Wembley jinx!

learning something new all the time. They were always prepared to stop and pass on their experience to the other players.

But when it came down to first-team places they had the midfield sown up between them. There was no way that a youngster like myself could compete.

So, because of the strong competition for places in the midfield, I was asked to provide cover in the left-back spot. But yet again the route to the first-team was blocked by an international player — Chris Hughton.

Eventually, having started only 14 League games in six years, I knew I would have to move to another club to further my career. So, when Norwich City showed an interest, I had to take the opportunity.

Carrow Road had already provided a new base for two old friends from Tottenham — Ian Culverhouse and Ian

Crook so I knew quite a bit about the club. The two Ians had told me that Norwich were a team who like to play in a similar style to that at White Hart Lane. That meant concentrating on a passing game, which suited me fine.

Having signed for Norwich, the first question that had to be answered was about my position. Did they want me as a midfielder or a left-back? Well, I think the boss at the time, Ken Brown, did have me marked out as a midfielder, but I managed to persuade him that the best bet would be to put me at left-back instead.

That was agreed and for the first time in my career I looked set for regular football in Division One. At the same time it would help my international ambitions with Wales.

There's no doubt that my career really took off as soon as I went to Norwich. In my second season with the

ROBERT FLECK
Norwich City

LEE CHAPMAN
Leeds United

WHAT A YEAR

for Nottingham Forest's bright new star ROY KEANE.

WHEN Roy Keane scored the second Nottingham Forest goal in last season's FA Cup semi-final against West Ham United, effectively booking his team's passage to Wembley, he may well have remembered one he hit round about twelve months earlier.

Playing for League of Ireland side Cobh Ramblers, the midfielder found the net against Monaghan United in a Republic of Ireland Cup-tie. The crowd that day was 202!

The one he fired in at Villa Park to help Forest to a 4-0 win and a date with Tottenham Hotspur in the Final was witnessed by over 40,000 in the stadium, plus a television viewing

GARY CROSBY

STEVE HODGE

THAT WAS . . .

figure in excess of 15,000,000 in this country alone.

The two goals summed up what the 20-year-old has achieved in just over a year in English football.

He became a regular in Brian Clough's first team after just ten minutes in the club's reserve side, finished third in the Young Player of the Year Poll conducted by the Professional Footballers' Association, progressed to a place in Jack Charlton's Republic of Ireland team, and played in the FA Cup Final.

Clough was so impressed with the kid who cost him just £15,000 that he decided he was good enough to make his League debut against Liverpool at Anfield! Roy takes up the story.

"I had a couple of trial periods with Forest and signed for them in May, 1990. Brian Clough didn't see me during my first week's trial so I returned later for another stint.

"I'd been training full-time in Ireland under their equivalent of the YTS scheme. I'd been unemployed and the course I went on paid me something like £50 a week.

"I'd wanted to break into English football and Forest were the first club to express an interest. Although one or two others approached me when they heard about my trial, I reckoned they were interested only because Forest were.

"I never considered moving elsewhere. Forest were so good to me during my initial stays there. It seemed a real family club.

"I went back to Ireland for the summer then reported for pre-season training and a tour with Forest's third team. All I was looking to do in my first season was to break into the reserve team.

"The tour went well and I was named as substitute for the first reserve team match. The manager was in the stand watching but left before I was brought on, ten minutes from the end.

"The next day I reported to the ground to be told by Forest's assistant manager Ron Fenton that he was driving me up to Liverpool to join the first-team squad preparing for the League game at Anfield. The idea was that I would meet the senior players and be 16th man for the game. That meant taking my boots along.

"An hour before kick-off Brian

Clough told me I was playing! I couldn't believe it. If I'd known the day before, I'd never have got to sleep.

"I guess that's the way the boss knew it would be and why he told me so late. He kept the pressure off me.

"Playing your first game in English football at Anfield is really something. After appearing in front of crowds of a few hundred in the League of Ireland, stepping out in front of 33,000 was unbelievable.

"After the game I stayed in the side for the rest of the season. The standard of football was obviously much higher than I'd been used to, so I had no choice but to adapt quickly.

"I did feel I might drop out of the line-up once England midfield man Steve Hodge was fit again. He had a lot of niggly injuries over the course of the campaign and many people thought I was in just because he wasn't available.

"Steve and I are very similar in style. We both like to get forward from the middle and have a pot at goal. It surprised me that when he was fit, I stayed in alongside him.

"The funny thing was that I scored eleven goals during the campaign and

they all came when Steve was out injured. When he was in the side, he was the one doing the scoring.

"I don't believe that's anything but coincidence. Playing alongside him, I still get into the opposition penalty-box.

"Because I scored a few goals for Forest in my first season, people are surprised when I tell them I scored only once in League of Ireland football. I certainly wasn't classed as a goalscoring midfield player.

"That I've become one is down to the way Forest play. I seem to get so many chances."

BRIAN CLOUGH ON KEANE

"The last player to give me such a boost was Gary Crosby. He lifted my heart and kept me in the game for another couple of years.

"It could be that Keane will keep me in the game a bit longer because it's some time since I felt so right about a player.

"I saw him for 20 minutes in a pre-season friendly and couldn't believe how good he was. When we were in a bit of a spot and I needed someone at Liverpool I had no doubts about him at all. It might have raised some eyebrows among my coaching staff, but that's their problem.

"He's got a great character and is a very level-headed young man with a very bright future."

23

ERIC YOUNG
Crystal Palace

NIGEL CLOUGH
Nottingham Forest

25

YOU CAN'T BEAT A GOOD SCRAP!

MANCHESTER CITY'S DAVID WHITE LIKES A GOOD SCRAP ON THE PITCH — AND OFF IT, AS WELL!

What a load of rubbish! That's not the type of chant a footballer likes to hear. Manchester City's David White is no exception . . . when he's on the pitch for the Maine Road side that is.

Off the field, however, the England B international is more than happy to hear that 'rubbish' cry because the 23-year-old spends his spare time away from football in the family's scrap metal and waste disposal businesses.

While most soccer stars like to relax on the golf course away from the pressures of football, White winds down by tackling the accounts!

David became involved in the family concern when his father, Stewart, asked if he was interested in making use of the spare time a footballer's life can offer.

The main family business is a scrap metal and industrial waste disposal company. David's father also owns properties which are rented out and David's first job was to collect 18 weeks' back rent

from a take-away!

In the last couple of years David has become co-owner of a smaller firm with his brother Steve. They bought a wagon and deal in mini-skips for domestic waste. David's main role is to keep the company accounts in order.

"It may sound anything but relaxing, but I really enjoy it," says the winger. "I can't play golf so I find this takes my mind off football and helps me to relax away from the game.

"I work two afternoons a week and a full day depending on my footballing schedule with City. I don't see myself staying in football after I have finished playing so this is a very good grounding for me."

SANDWICHED

Eire's PAUL McGRATH is the man in the middle between England's DAVID PLATT and TONY ADAMS.
Hard to believe that Paul and David are club mates at Villa!

GEORGE PARRIS
West Ham

28

BRIAN GRANT
Aberdeen

MOVING from one country to another is a slow job in football as I found out before I arrived in England. I didn't know too much about Luton Town when I first came here — they weren't a big name in Denmark, my home country.

English football is seen on TV in Denmark but it's usually big teams like Liverpool, Manchester United and Arsenal that are shown. Luton were an unknown quality — except for the occasional player I had heard of such as Steve Foster and Mick Harford.

For several months I had heard about the possibility of moving to various different clubs, in a number of countries. Agents, managers and journalists were all phoning me to say I was going to such and such a club, in one country or another.

At the time I was playing for OB Odense in Denmark knowing that it was time for a fresh start in my career. I wanted to play in a league of a higher standard than Denmark's.

At one stage I started to talk to the German club Nuremberg. That would have been an interesting move but it didn't quite work out. So I had to keep looking until the right club came along.

Eventually I discovered that Luton Town were the club most interested in signing me. That's a very important factor when you are considering a move. The manager at the time was Ray Harford and he'd decided he wanted me just by watching me on TV and on videos.

If he was prepared to take a gamble on me then I was happy to sign for the club. After months of speculation and doubt, I was on my way at last — to England.

That meant I had to brush up on my English. I could speak the language a bit — but that didn't mean I was going to be able to understand what the Luton players were saying!

The best way to make myself understood was by doing a job on the pitch. After a couple of games as sub to settle in, the third game saw me picked from the off. I was on my way!

It didn't take me long to get amongst the goals and I was really beginning to enjoy life in the Football League when disaster struck. A bad knee injury meant I had to go in to hospital for three days after Christmas 1989 for a cartilage operation. That's the last thing I wanted so soon after coming to England.

At first, I was optimistic that it

SLOW MOTION TRANSFER

Luton's Danish star LARS ELSTRUP tells the tale

wouldn't be too long before I was back in the game but unfortunately the operation wasn't successful. I had to go back in to hospital for a second operation just a couple of months later. I was very frustrated that everything seemed to be going wrong in my opening season at Luton.

To make matters worse, my new team-mates were starting to struggle in the League and I was also missing out on international football as Denmark tried, in vain, to qualify for the 1990 World Cup Finals.

I had been third choice striker for my country — playing quite a few games but sitting on the bench for a lot more. One moment of glory for me though was scoring against England when Peter Shilton was making his record-breaking appearance for them.

After months of frustration, I got myself back as substitute for Luton's final four games of the 1989-90 season. At that stage, things looked so vital to the future of the club. In the end it all came down to the last game of the season at Derby.

It was a game we had to win to avoid relegation. We couldn't have made a better start either — after 20 minutes we were already 2-0 up.

But Derby came back at us and by half-time they'd levelled the scores at 2-2. We were just 45 minutes away from dropping into Division Two. Things were beginning to look desperate when, 15 minutes from the end, Kingsley Black scored the winning goal to keep us in the

top flight.

What a relief! Having missed so much of the season with the injury, it would have been terrible to see the team get relegated. Survival meant I had the chance to make a fresh start to my career in the English

KINGSLEY BLACK

First Division. I was determined to make up for lost time.

The new campaign couldn't have started better. I found myself quickly amongst the goals — particularly away from home. I was having some very profitable away trips, but struggling to get on the scoresheet at Kenilworth Road.

Like any striker, goals are important to me but I don't regard them as being the only part of my game. I certainly don't take much interest in how I'm doing in the goal-charts compared with Ian Rush or Gary Lineker.

I play a lot of my football in a wide position, either down the right or left flank. That gives me the chance to find a lot of different goal-scoring positions and to surprise opponents.

I feel much happier when I'm able to take on defenders, as well as cutting in to have shots. My strength is one of my best qualities and I like to think I have a good shot with my left foot as well.

When I first came to Luton, I was expected to play like a target man in place of Mick Harford. That meant playing with my back to the opponents' goal all the time and I have to say that never suited me.

There were lots of things to get used to when I first came to England. The language, a different style of football, playing on the plastic pitch Luton had at the time. I expected a lot of myself very quickly.

But now I've got used to England — I plan on sticking around for a while yet.

BRIAN MARWOOD
Sheffield United

ANDERS LIMPAR *Arsenal*

33

I'M WALKING

ROGER JOSEPH

WHEN I ran out at Vicarage Road for my England B debut against Iceland last April I had to laugh at the irony of the situation. There I was, about to start an international match, at the very ground where, as a 14-year-old, I'd been rejected as being too small!

Watford was the perfect place for me to get my first taste of the international scene. After all, when I left there as a kid my chances of ever becoming a professional footballer didn't look too good.

Another satisfied man in the crowd that day was Watford's kit-man, Ken Brooks, who had been the scout responsible for taking me to the club. He'd nearly resigned when he heard I wasn't being kept on. He could afford to smile when he saw me playing for England B!

England boss, Graham Taylor, had been the manager at Watford when I was there, so it was good to know he had noticed my progress. Being selected for that game made me realise just how quickly my career had moved. Two years previously I'd been playing non-League football for East London club, Leytonstone Ilford.

With an England squad, everything is laid on. The training facilities are good, you work with top coaches and stay in the best hotels.

It was different in my non-League days. Then I played at some rough grounds with very ordinary facilities. That background certainly made me appreciate my England opportunity all the more.

I'd orginally drifted into the non-League game after serving an apprenticeship at Leyton Orient. I didn't do badly at Brisbane Road but the verdict was the same as before — 'you're too small to make it in this game'.

But, fortunately, in my late teens I grew a few more vital inches and I eventually got another chance with a League club when Maidstone signed me before their first-ever season in Division Four. That was an exciting year to be at Maidstone, because everything was new to the club and the players.

That euphoria helped us gain fifth position and a place in the end-of-season play-offs. But then Cambridge beat us to end our chance of reaching Division Three.

My own disappointment was short-lived. Within a few weeks of the end of the season, I had signed for Wimbledon and was on the brink of a career in Division One. Again things were happening so quickly.

I couldn't have chosen more appropriate opponents than Arsenal to make my League debut. As a kid, I had been a big Gunners fan, as had my father and his father before him.

But I had turned my back on the chance of a career at Highbury when I chose to go to Watford. Arsenal was such a big club that I really couldn't see that I was going to make an impression there.

Several players who have been a part of Arsenal's success in recent years were in the very early stages of their Highbury careers then — Tony Adams, David Rocastle, Paul Merson, Michael Thomas all came up through the ranks. Even now I wonder whether I would have made it at Arsenal against that sort of competition.

They certainly showed what good players they had become during my debut for Wimbledon. They beat us 3-0 that day and by the end of the season I was cheering them on to the championship.

I couldn't have had a tougher baptism in Division One, but I wasn't going to let it put me off.

There would be plenty of good things to look forward to in the season ahead.

When I first arrived at Plough Lane, I expected to be playing at right-back. That was where I felt most comfortable, especially when it looked as if the regular number two — Roger Joseph — would be leaving the club.

But manager Ray Harford had other ideas. He wanted to make the most of what you might call my 'good engine' and play me on the right-side of midfield with

TALL NOW!

Roger keeping the right-back slot. I'm not the fastest sprinter at the club but when it comes to stamina I'm in my element, as I show over the cross-country training runs.

The boss's plan worked well. After a shaky start when neither of us seemed to know what we should be doing, we began to develop a very professional understanding. I could provide Roger with the support he needed with defensive duties, and he would help me out when we were on the attack.

It doesn't always run smoothly, of course. I don't suppose there

a ground where I'd never been before.

Highbury, White Hart Lane and Old Trafford were all places to add to my list last season, but the most memorable personal moment came in January at Anfield.

Liverpool were in hot pursuit of Arsenal at the top of the table at the time and John Barnes had scored a first-half goal that looked like giving them the three points.

But, as most teams know to their cost, Wimbledon never give up and we certainly weren't going to let them win without a fight. We

Wimbledon's
WARREN BARTON
has plenty to be pleased about.

are many games when we don't argue with each other about who should have done what. But that just keeps us on our toes to do the job properly.

The final proof of how well that partnership worked last season came when we lined up together in that England B game against Iceland.

Graham Taylor and his assistant, Lawrie McMenemy, made it clear that they wanted to develop the best possible team at international level — not just select the most talented eleven individuals. So, if you could prove you fit into his style of play, you had a chance with England.

I've always thought of myself as an adaptable sort of player so I'd like to think I will stay in the reckoning over the next few seasons. But, despite that versatility, I still think that my long-term future will be at right-back. I really think I could be one of the best around in that position.

Last season was certainly a time for learning quickly and taking in a whole range of new experiences. Nearly every week I found myself playing against a team for the first time, or going to

stormed back in the second-half determined to get an equalisr.

Just nine minutes were left on the clock when I got the chance to make a name for myself in front of the Kop. We were awarded a free-kick about 25 yards out from Bruce Grobbelaar's goal and Terry Gibson came up and said I should give it a go.

I made my mind up straightaway — I was going to keep the ball as low as possible and bend it round the wall with my right foot. As I approached the ball I just kept that picture in my mind — keep the ball low.

I never saw the ball hit the back of the net — the rest of the lads just engulfed me! At that moment I became a hero.

My first proper look at that goal came on the TV highlights the next day — and I made sure I caught it on video. Ever since, whenever I've felt a bit low in confidence, I've taken a look at that video, or the one of our 5-1 win against Tottenham, and it works wonders. I soon feel ready to go out and play well again.

After that goal at Anfield I was soon walking tall. Nobody could say that I was too small for football anymore!

OVER MY SHOULDER . . .

Manchester City's Niall Quinn makes a back for Manchester United's Gary Pallister.

DES WALKER *Nottingham Forest*

IN THE HOT SEAT!

Everton midfielder JOHN EBBRELL faces the questions — and gives his answers.

WHEN DID YOU FIRST WANT TO BE A PROFESSIONAL FOOTBALLER?

My family are all football fans and they encouraged me from a young age. My father supported Liverpool and he often took me to Anfield to watch the Reds. I must admit my father's influence caused me to support Liverpool as a kid, but I can assure all Evertonians that my allegiance changed as soon as I came to Everton.

DID YOU PLAY FOR YOUR SCHOOL TEAM?

I represented my junior school in Liverpool. But my secondary school was 'rugby-only' and there was no opportunity to play organised games there. However, I made up for that by playing in a Sunday League team.

HOW DID YOU GAIN A PLACE IN THE F.A. NATIONAL SCHOOL AT LILLESHALL?

I was 14 years old and going to Everton on Monday nights for training. The club heard about a new initiative by the Football Association called the 'School of Excellence' and advised me to ask my parents to apply to be a pupil. As you can imagine, there was great competition for places and I went through a series of trials before I was accepted.

WHAT DID THE F.A. NATIONAL SCHOOL ENTAIL?

I was on the inaugural scheme which lasted between 1984-86. The class consisted of 22 boys who had all showed football skills as youngsters. The school combines normal academic duties with football. It concentrates on basic skills, and that means improving touch and awareness about the game. Dave Sexton was the England Under-21 coach and was in charge of our training as well. We also had instruction from various regional coaches and present England boss Graham Taylor also coached us. Our health and fitness improved as a result of eating a proper diet and daily exercise.

DID YOU GET HOMESICK LIVING AWAY FROM LIVERPOOL?

Lilleshall is nearly 100 miles from my parents' home, so I had to live in accommodation at the school. Leaving home at such a young age was a difficult thing to do. Most of the pupils were away from home for the first time and especially during the first eight weeks we all felt very homesick. But we got over it.

DID YOU EVER GET FED UP WITH TOO MUCH FOOTBALL?

At 14, you never get fed up playing football. Anyway, I'd probably have been spending more time kicking a football in the park if I hadn't been at Lilleshall. We came home from school and we were out on the field by four-thirty. We'd have tea at six o'clock then it was down to homework, so it wasn't very different to a normal school day. Although it was a school designed to help budding footballers, there wasn't too much football involved.

WHO ARE YOUR IDOLS?

When I was a youngster I admired Liverpool and England striker Kevin Keegan, and more recently Manchester United and England midfielder Bryan Robson. Both players are tremendous enthusiasts for the game and as well as being strong and skilful on the ball, could motivate their team-mates.

DO YOU MODEL YOURSELF ON ANY PLAYER?

No! When I go to watch games I look at the good parts of a player's game and try to put that into my game. I feel that if you try and model yourself on any particular player then it's unlikely you can be as successful as that player. We all have individual skills and parts of our game that we are comfortable with but others wouldn't be.

WHAT HAPPENED AFTER YOU GRADUATED FROM THE F.A. NATIONAL SCHOOL?

Three days after I graduated on July 8, 1986, I started an apprenticeship at Everton and began the long, hard slog to try to prove that all I learned in the school was worthwhile.

WHO WERE THE BIGGEST INFLUENCES AT EVERTON?

Without doubt Peter Reid (now player-boss of Manchester City) and Paul Bracewell (now Sunderland) were big influences when I was an apprentice at Everton and learning my trade. They always made themselves available if I wanted advice, and I also admired the amount of work they put in for Everton on and off the park.

CAN YOU REMEMBER YOUR DEBUT FOR EVERTON?

Yes! It was against Charlton Athletic in the Full Members Cup on March 2, 1987. I came on as sub for the second-half. The match was tied at 2-2 after extra-time and went to penalties. Although I scored in the penalty shoot-out we lost .   My League debut didn't come until February 4, 1989 against Wimbledon at Goodison Park. The game finished 1-1.

HAVE YOU ENGLAND REPRESENTATIVE HONOURS?

I have been fortunate to represent England at all levels except full internationals. It's always a great honour to pull on the national jersey and recently I've also been handed the captaincy of the Under-21 side. Hopefully, one day I can lead out the full England side at Wembley. Although I admit that is probably some way off yet.

WHAT ARE YOUR AMBITIONS IN THE GAME?

First and foremost, to stay clear of serious injury. There have been many great players who have had their career cut short through injury. After that, I hope to maintain a regular place in the Everton side and be a part of a championship-winning side. In the future I would like to captain my club and country.

PETER REID

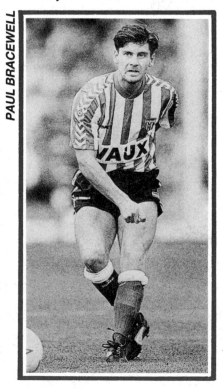

PAUL BRACEWELL

COLLISION COURSE!

There's no holding back when Damian Matthew (Chelsea) meets Manchester United's Paul Ince in a tussle for possession.

ROY WEGERLE
Queen's Park Rangers

41

IAN ORMONDROYD (Aston Villa)

BRIAN McCLAIR (Manchester United)

STEVE NICOL (Liverpool)

Question — When does Andy become Officer, David become Bugsy and Owen become Blackadder?
Answer — On the football field.

THE N[GAME

They are all nicknames given to players by team-mates or supporters. Every player has a nickname, but not all of them are as interesting as those above. While it's obvious why Paul Gascoigne is Gazza and Bryan Robson answers to Robbo, the origins of other nicknames aren't so easy to fathom. For example, how did Leeds' star Mel Sterland come by the nickname of The Fonz?

That's from a likeness Elland Road supporters noticed between the full-back and The Fonz, the star of TV's Happy Days. Similarly Manchester City's Andy Dibble gets his nickname of Officer from the policeman Officer Dibble in the Boss Cat cartoon. John Barnes is another television tie-up. He's known as Digger Barnes at Anfield, taken from the character of the same name in the popular soap opera Dallas.

Nothing so glamorous for former Celtic man and current Barnsley star Owen Archdeacon, though. The Oakwell regulars know him as Blackadder, a reference to what they think is a likeness between him and funnyman Rowan Atkinson.

Nottingham Forest and England full-back Stuart Pearce looks nothing like the star of the Psycho films Anthony Perkins. But his ruthless approach towards opposition wingers has earned him the title Psycho, a nickname that has since been picked up by several other hard men. The no-nonsense approach adopted by Wimbledon's John Fashanu gave him the Fash The Bash tag.

Former Arsenal and West Ham

hero Liam Brady had a real liking for food — especially chips. This led to him being labelled Chippy, a name which has remained even though he no longer plays.

But Liverpool's Steve Nicol continues the food link through his alias of Chopsy. Anfield gave him this tag because of his hunger for fish, chips and crisps.

Team-mate David Burrows hasn't escaped the Reds' mickey-takers either. Having his surname he was bound to be given some kind of rabbit-related nickname. He's known as Bugs or Bugsy after the world's most famous bunny.

Liverpool's rivals Manchester United also have alternative titles for their players. Brian McClair is known as Choccy because his surname resembles an eclair, that tasty chocolate pastry.

Everyone knows Mark Hughes as

CKNAME

**ROY AITKEN
(ex-Newcastle)**

Sparky, but to many it's a mystery as to where it originated. It's derived from another nickname, Marks and Sparks, given to the Marks and Spencers stores.

United's Manchester rivals City have Peter Reid at the helm, otherwise known as Fred. This comes from his likeness to comedian Freddie Starr. But during his time at Everton he was known as Fred Two. This was because Andy Gray was thought to look more like Starr and he was labelled Fred One.

Another Maine Road man, Adrian Heath, is known as Inchy. This stems from his time at Stoke and is a reference to his height of five feet six inches.

Stoke star Wayne Biggins came to be called Bertie in a rather unusual way. He decided he wasn't keen on being called Wayne and asked his team-mates to call him anything but that. Bertie was the name they came up with and it's stayed with the striker ever since.

Derby County's Gerraint Williams has also swapped his first name for an alternative. It isn't a case of the Welsh international not being keen on Gerraint, just that his Rams' team-mates found it difficult to pronounce. From that day on everyone has referred to him as George.

Baseball Ground team-mate Ted McMinn has been known as Tin Man since his Rangers days. This was derived from his strange running action, said by the Ibrox fans to resemble the Tin Man from The Wizard of Oz.

Sheffield Wednesday's Viv Anderson stops opposition forwards with an extension of one of his ultra long legs. It's that trick that earned him the name Spider.

Roy Aitken was always The Bear at Celtic, a reference to his size and his hunger for the battle. But he also had a much more meek nickname in Shirley. This was because of his curly locks, similar

to those sported by 1930's film star Shirley Temple.

Celtic star Dariusz Wdowczyk has the kind of name even fellow Poles would have difficulty with. Celtic fans couldn't manage it either so they decided to give him

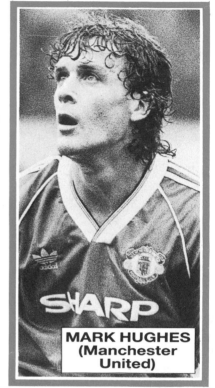

**MARK HUGHES
(Manchester
United)**

an adopted Scottish name. He's now known as Shuggy, a Scots version of Hugh.

A guppy certainly isn't Scottish, it's a tropical fish. It's also the nickname of Sheffield United's Mark Morris. He resembles former Wimbledon and Crewe man Paul Fishenden, predictably known as Fish. But team-mates at Bramall Lane decided to be a bit more exotic and so gave him the tag Guppy.

Brian Clough may not come across as being very jolly, but his City Ground star Steve Hodge is completely the opposite. Cloughie refers to his England international midfielder as Happy Harry because he's always smiling. If Aston Villa's Ian Ormondroyd was smiling you probably wouldn't be able to tell. The striker is so tall and thin his head seems to be in the clouds. His lanky physique led to his former Bradford City pals naming him Stick.

Tony Philliskirk and David Reeves look very much alike. Both Bolton Wanderers men are tall and blonde, just like pop twins Matt and Luke Goss, also known as Bros. It wasn't long before the two of them were being called Bros around their Burnden Park ground.

GORDON DURIE
Chelsea

44

JOHN DREYER
Luton

45

Stars from the Continent have become an accepted part of the English scene. Here some of the imports talk about the experiences in England.

NAYIM

HOW DID YOU COME TO BE PLAYING IN ENGLAND?

NAYIM (TOTTENHAM HOTSPUR): When Johann Cruyff took over from Terry Venables at Barcelona he made it clear that I didn't figure in his plans. He said, 'You're not playing for me because you're not fit enough.' Meanwhile, Mr Venables had been given the manager's job at White Hart Lane. He invited me over and I accepted right away.

GLENN HYSEN (LIVERPOOL): I was playing in Italy with Fiorentina, but was very unhappy. I could hardly speak Italian at all for the first year. I wanted a way out and Manchester United were rumoured to be interested. In the end they hesitated and Kenny Dalglish moved in and brought me to Anfield.

GLENN HYSEN

KEN MONKOU (CHELSEA): Bobby Campbell, the Chelsea manager, spotted me playing for Feyenoord in Holland, when he was watching the Australian striker Dave Mitchell. I had come through the youth side at Feyenoord with several other young players, but because we didn't cost anything we always had to make way for the big-money signings. I felt I was being denied a real chance to establish myself in the team.

ROLAND NILSSON (SHEFFIELD WEDNESDAY): I had been at Gothenburg for seven years and I needed a change. I wanted especially to come to England. I was excited when Manchester United offered me a trial, but while I was in England, Wednesday offered me a firm contract. It was an easy choice to make and I signed right away.

KENT NIELSEN

KENT NIELSEN (ASTON VILLA): I was with Brondby in Denmark before moving here. I was 27, had won League Championship medals and played in the Cup Final in Denmark. There was no new challenge on the horizon. Because of my size, I thought the English game would suit me best.

LUDEK MIKLOSKO (WEST HAM): I was the goalie at Banik Ostrava and was brought over here by Billy Bonds as a replacement for Phil Parkes, who sadly had to retire because of injury.

BJORN KRISTENSEN (NEWCASTLE UNITED): I was playing in defence with Aarhus in Denmark. I thought it would be a good career move if I could come over and play in the English League, and hopefully win promotion with Newcastle.

WHAT BIG DIFFERENCES ARE THERE IN THE GAME IN ENGLAND?

NIELSEN: The pace is much more hectic. You have to be tough to survive in England. I'm not saying the game is dirtier here, but on the Continent a defender can win the ball in a tackle and then have time to look around before making a pass. It's not often the player you've just beaten attempts to regain possession. In English soccer they keep coming back at you.

MIKLOSKO: The game here is played at a much faster pace than I was used to, and there are many more matches. We also had a mid-season break from December to February in Czechoslovakia, but I like being involved all the time.

HYSEN: In Italy there are four or five top teams, the rest are really there just to make up the numbers. I knew when I moved here it would be tough against the top sides like Arsenal, Manchester United and Tottenham, but at the same time I expected it to be easy against most of the others. I was very wrong!

MONKOU: In Holland the players train a lot longer. Twice a day, six days a week. Here there are more matches, but I still have more free time. At first it took a lot of getting used to, but now I like it. I would rather play than train anyway.

KRISTENSEN: In Denmark I joined a football club when I was six years old. Even at that age I was taught tactics and how to play possession football. British kids just kick a football around the streets, and it shows in the way the two countries play professional soccer. You have to be 100 per cent fit to play in England, whereas on the Continent you could get away with being 85 per cent fit because there's a lot less running to do.

WERE THERE ANY MAJOR DIFFERENCES OFF THE PITCH?

HYSEN: It was crazy in Italy. If the team won you were a god. You could go into the shops the following week and buy goods at half price. But if we lost, the fans threw stones at us!

NILSSON: Here I'm a full-time footballer. In Sweden you have to have a job to supplement your income. The last thing you want to do after a bad day at work is run all over a football pitch for ninety minutes!

MIKLOSKO: Back in Czechoslovakia it was almost impossible to go on a foreign holiday because of the price, and here there is a much wider range of goods in the shops. Also, in the winter here my wife and I still see children going to school in short trousers. To us that defies logic!

KRISTENSEN: There is a lot more pressure put on players by the supporters and the Press. Football is life and death to fans here in the north-east. In Denmark we don't have fans, just people who watch matches.

DID YOU ENCOUNTER ANY MAJOR PROBLEMS ON YOUR ARRIVAL IN ENGLAND?

NAYIM: The hardest part for me was the language. Football is international. You can always make yourself understood on the pitch, but in the dressing-room it's a different matter. All the players laughed at my

attempts to learn English. I couldn't understand Gazza but I knew he was always making fun of me!

NIELSEN: I found the pace of the game shattering. I felt very tired after matches, and it was no surprise to me when the then-manager Graham Taylor dropped me from the team. I just did not have the stamina. But when I was dropped I trained morning, afternoon and evening to get back in!

KRISTENSEN: Soon after I joined Newcastle, I wanted away. I was not playing regularly in the first team and I was unhappy. However, I didn't want to rock the boat by asking for a transfer request because United had just paid £250,000 for me. That may not sound like much in this country, but in Denmark it's a big fee.

MIKLOSKO: I came to England without knowing a single word of English. I couldn't understand the people, the newspapers or the TV. But I expected things to be difficult, and I think I'm coping.

DID YOU FIND IT DIFFICULT TO SETTLE IN?

NIELSEN: Graham Taylor deserves credit for helping me through my first months over here. He was very understanding about the problems I faced. For example, the new lifestyle and having to spend two months in a hotel in a foreign country. My wife and I ran up a huge 'phone bill telephoning family and friends in Denmark!

NILSSON: Not really. I think I was playing the best football of my career before my ligament injury. Glenn Hysen and I are good friends too, so we often meet for a chat.

HYSEN: No. I felt at home right away. Liverpool are a superb club. The football and the social life both suited me. Compared to Italy, England is paradise!

NAYIM: I was lucky because team mates Gudni Bergsson, Erik Thortsvedt, Paul Stewart and Paul Gascoigne were all in the same hotel at the same time as me. So I wasn't surrounded by complete

strangers all the time. I took English lessons too, but the best way to learn is to just go out and talk to people. But I had to learn not to be embarrassed about making mistakes!

WHAT DO YOU THINK OF THE STANDARD OF ENGLISH FOOTBALL?

MIKLOSKO: I have always admired English football. It was always my ambition to play in the First Division here.

HYSEN: I have played in other Leagues with big stars, but this one is the best. I also have no doubt the best player in the world is Liverpool's John Barnes.

MONKOU: I don't think English football is given the credit it deserves for skill. I believe if I can play here competently, then I can play anywhere in the world.

NAYIM: Simply, the English League is the best in the world.

KEN MONKOU

MARCO GABBIADINI
Sunderland

TERRY PHELAN
Wimbledon

MANDY MADE HISTORY

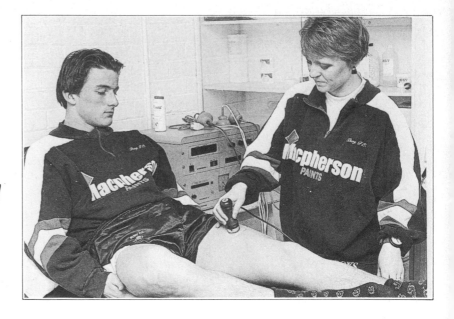

ASK any football fan who Mandy Johnson is and you will receive mostly blank stares. But asking nearer the vicinity of Bury FC will bring a smile of recognition. For Mandy is one of the club's background staff.

Nothing unusual in that you may think, but what makes Mandy's position unique is that she is the only female physio in the Football League!

Mandy was offered the job after being recommended to then-manager Sam Ellis by a mutual friend. Bury were without a full-time physiotherapist and needed a qualified person at short notice, so Mandy was asked to take the job on a month's trial. But, both she and Mr Ellis were unsure whether or not the move would work out at first.

"I had been working with professional and amateur sports people all around the country but had never been involved with a professional football team before," Mandy explains.

"I think the manager was a bit wary of giving the job to me, and I didn't know how the players would react. But sports-related injuries are my speciality and Mr Ellis was desperate at the time. He needed someone with the qualifications to do the job.

"It was very much new ground for everybody. Bury didn't know if I would be able to get on with the players, or they with me. So it was decided to have a trial period of one month to see how things went.

"However, I settled in right away. I think the players were all a little bit shocked initially when I walked in but there wasn't any hostility.

"I'm older than most of the players so I think they were more frightened of me than I was of them! Anyway, at the end of the week they want to be fit to play so basically they'll do anything I tell them!"

Being a woman in such a male-dominated world did not hold any fears for Mandy, who has practised physiotherapy with various athletics and swimming teams in London for a number of years. She looks upon it, quite rightly, as just another job. But being so outnumbered by the men can throw up some amusing incidents at times.

"I've come up against over-zealous club stewards a couple of times," she continues. "They've tried to prevent me from getting into the grounds and the players have had to come and rescue me by saying 'It's alright — she's with us!' But apart from those odd moments I enjoy this job tremendously.

"I'd like to see more women becoming involved in the game. But football is so male-dominated that many women aren't interested in the sport to start with. It also involves a lot of time and I think if I was married with children I would find it impossible to do this job.

"You really have to be willing to give up the time. I can't see many women wanting to do that if they had a family. I have no ties of that sort so the demands of the job don't present a problem to me."

The life of a football club's physio can certainly be hectic at times. Mandy has to work a demanding seven-day week. With 25 professionals plus trainees, on the books at Bury, there is usually someone needing treatment. Not much time is left aside for socialising, but Mandy says that has never bothered her.

She goes on, "With the opportunities which exist in this job I would not hesitate to encourage someone into it. With the right qualifications you have the chance to work all over the world. So it does have a good side too. When the time came for me to choose a career I always wanted to be a PE teacher or a physio and I'm still glad I made the choice I did.

"It is tiring. There are no week-ends off. As I've said it would be harder for me if I had a husband and children. But I've never been a 9-to-5 person. This job is a very satisfying one so I'm happy to accept the long hours."

Mandy is convinced more and more women will be involved in football in the near future.

She says, "Out of all the 92 clubs in the Football League there are surprisingly few who employ a qualified physio.

"With the amount of money these clubs are paying for players nowadays they want the very best treatment. There just aren't enough men to fill those posts, so eventually I think we'll see a lot more women doing my job."

Part of Mandy's task, of course, is to watch over the players during a game for signs of serious injury. Luckily she says these have been few and far between, and there have been no really damaging injuries in her time at Bury. Part of the job is also to know when the players are acting!

"I can tell right away if they're faking," she laughs. "Sometimes they'll say to me, 'It's alright, Mandy. I've just gone down for a breather.' They're soon get told to get back up and play!

"But the lads here are a good bunch and they usually won't try that. If anything they'll want to stay on and it will be me who has to insist they come off. That's the only time we have real disagreements.

"Working for a football team has been a great experience for me. Despite being a bit wary about the job at first, I'm glad I got the chance to give it a go," ends Mandy.

IT'S SO EASY . . .

It seems as if Liverpool's Bruce Grobbelaar has got things in the palm of his hand. Amazing what a spot of super glue can do!

51

STEVE BRUCE
Manchester United

DAVID HIRST
Sheffield Wednesday

DRAGONS

LEYTON ORIENT

THE STORIES BEHIND THE BADGES OF SOME FAMOUS CLUBS

NEWCASTLE UNITED

LEICESTER CITY

IT'S sometimes difficult trying to work out the origin of club emblems! Unless you are a supporter or live in the area, you may not realise the significance of, for instance, the little tower on the Everton emblem or the swift on the Walsall badge. Most badges, however, are straight forward and they tend to fall into three categories.

Many simply incorporate their town or city coat of arms into their badge such as Liverpool, Newcastle United and Burnley. Others have the club's initials interwoven on an attractive design and these include Leeds United and Queen's Park Rangers.

Another type of badge incorporates an animal or associated object and usually illustrates the club nickname. Among the clubs to adopt this idea are Leicester City, known as the 'Foxes' and Notts County who have the nickname of the 'Magpies'. Both clubs have those animals prominent on their emblem.

Another example is Nottingham Forest who changed from the city's coat of arms in 1973 to a tree with heraldic water underneath. This symbolises the club's last name, which is also their nickname, and the River Trent which flows near the club ground.

But other clubs have emblems that require a bit of explanation.

CHARLTON ATHLETIC have the design of a hand in a glove holding up a sword. This signifies the 'sword of the valiant' and represents their nickname 'The Valiants'. This tag from their home ground, The Valley, which they returned to in the summer after spending five seasons sharing Selhurst Park with Crystal Palace.

SCUNTHORPE UNITED recently changed their club badge from a fist grasping a chain, and replaced it with the Coat of Arms of Glanford Borough Council — the owners of their Glanford Park stadium. The club feared the original badge might have been seen by some people as a symbol of violence at a time when football hooliganism was common. However, the five links in the chain actually symbolised the five districts in the town and the fist holding the chain represented the togetherness of the town.

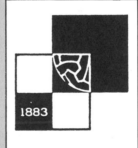

NOTTS COUNTY

NOTTINGHAM FOREST

BRISTOL ROVERS

PORT VALE

LEYTON ORIENT have two dragons facing each other with a football between them. They are Chinese dragons with an obvious reference to the Far East and, in particular, the Orient. The old badge had just one dragon but was changed in the early eighties because, according to a club spokesman, "it's better to have two dragons breathing fire than just one."

GILLINGHAM have a rampant horse on their badge. It signifies 'Kent Invicta' which is the logo for Kent. The club's nickname, 'The Gills' is interwoven in the horse's mane.

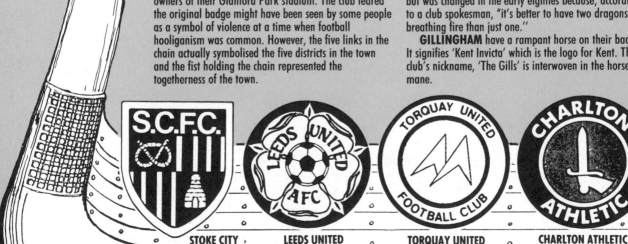

STOKE CITY   **LEEDS UNITED**   **TORQUAY UNITED**   **CHARLTON ATHLETIC**

HORSES and A VIKING...

DONCASTER ROVERS

IPSWICH TOWN

LIVERPOOL

NORTHAMPTON TOWN

GILLINGHAM

BURNLEY

EVERTON

DONCASTER ROVERS for many years didn't have a club emblem. In the late 1940s the local paper designed a figure wearing a red and white hooped jersey. It looked a bit like a pirate but the club failed to adopt it as the club emblem. It wasn't until Maurice Setters became manager in 1971 that the club decided to have a logo. Setters asked an art teacher friend to make a design and the result is a Viking . . .

EVERTON have a little tower prominent on their badge. The building is a popular landmark in the area and is a mile from the club's Goodison Park ground. The tower was formerly a debtors prison. The Latin legend at the bottom of the emblem 'Nil Satis Nisi Optimum' — is translated as 'Only Best Is Good Enough'.

BRISTOL ROVERS club badge is a recent design which has two interlocking squares. One square is blue with part of a football in the bottom left corner and the other square is quartered blue and white — the design of the club strip. A club spokesman called it "the most simple one in the Football League."

NORTHAMPTON TOWN have a relatively new logo and its design may have confused a few people. Above the NFC inscription a football boot can be seen kicking a giant football. A spokesman for the club agreed that, at first glance, it looks more like a key.

TORQUAY UNITED are another side with a modern — and some would say perplexing logo — for their club badge. The two strange objects are actually the wings of a seagull in flight. That's taken from the club's nickname, 'The Gulls'.

MANCHESTER CITY have a ship on their emblem in recognition of the Manchester Ship Canal which was opened by Queen Victoria in 1894 — the year the club changed its name from Ardwick FC to Manchester City.

PORT VALE and **STOKE CITY** have emblems that use objects prominent in the history of Staffordshire. The Staffordshire knot can be seen on both logos as can a bottle made in a kiln which symbolises that the clubs are situated in the Potteries.

IPSWICH TOWN are another club with a horse prominent on their club badge. The horse is a Suffolk Punch, the working horse of the East Anglian county. The wavy lines at the bottom of the emblem denote the river in the town and the portcullis at the top symbolises the gates Cardinal Wolsey created for the town's college.

WALSALL have a swift as their emblem and its connection dates back to the last century. The Midlands club played as Walsall Town Swifts until 1895, but although there is now no reference to the Swift in their title, the club badge is a strong reminder of the past.

MANCHESTER CITY

SCUNTHORPE UNITED

WALSALL

QUEEN'S PARK RANGERS

STEVE REDMOND
Manchester City

MO JOHNSTON *Rangers*

THEY HAD DON TAPED!

How DON HUTCHISON won a dream move — thanks to a video!

DON HUTCHISON is a name that could go down in history. Not that Liverpool's £175,000 signing from Hartlepool last season has broken any footballing records — yet. It's just that he was the first soccer buy made via video tape!

A video of Hartlepool's two-legged Rumbelows Cup second round tie with star-studded Spurs last term was sent to all First and Second Division club managers by the enterprising Victoria Ground chairman Gary Gibson.

Youngster Don had performances against the likes of Gascoigne, Lineker and Mabbutt, good enough to prompt Gibson and his manager Cyril Knowles to try to sell one of their prize assets to ease 'Pool's financial problems.

"I knew nothing about the video tape, nor about the move until it all happened," says 20-year-old Gateshead-born Don. "I didn't even realise a tape had been made of the game, never mind sent out to all the clubs.

"The first thing I knew was when Hartlepool manager Cyril Knowles phoned me at home to tell me that the then Liverpool manager Kenny Dalglish wanted to speak to me.

"I didn't know what to think or make of the news. That was until I went down to Anfield the following day. There Mr Dalglish told me that he wanted to sign me. I had no hesitation in saying 'yes'. Everything had happened so quickly.

"But no sooner had I put pen to paper than Kenny Dalglish asked me if I could play in a reserve team game the following evening. All I had with me were my boots and the clothes I stood in.

"But I certainly wasn't going to turn down the chance of playing and so I stayed on Merseyside for the evening. After that Mr Dalglish suggested I stay on for the rest of the week. I got by through borrowing clothes from the rest of the lads."

Don waited patiently for his chance throughout his first campaign at Anfield. The tall Geordie was labelled as a direct replacement for Alan Hansen when the talented Scot retired last season — if only because the two share a similar physique. But Don is quick to knock back comparisons.

"I think I was only really compared to Alan Hansen because I have played a few games at centre-half.

"While I was at Hartlepool I played in midfield and people said I was the new Paul Gascoigne. If I had been playing at centre-forward they would probably have labelled me the new Ian Rush," jokes Don.

"But my real position is in the midfield, even though I was handed a completely new role when I joined Liverpool. They told me I was a centre-half midfield player . . . a similar role to the one Alan Hansen played.

"Whatever, my big ambition now is to be a regular in the Liverpool team."

In a few years time, Don could be thanking a video tape for setting him on the way to the top.

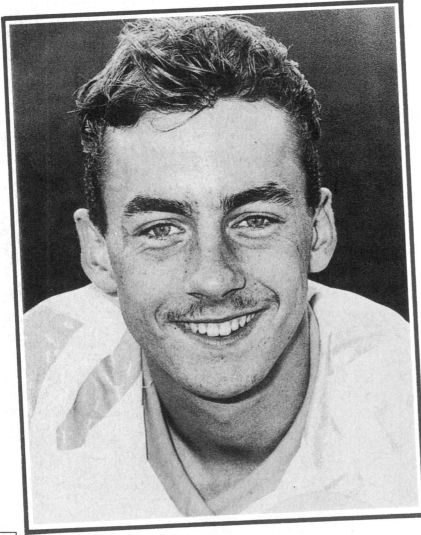

WITH A DIFFERENCE

IT WAS WORTH THE WAIT . . .

. . . so says Sheffield Wednesday's American star JOHN HARKES

JOHN HARKES certainly has one of the most unusual stories in the English Football League. Sheffield Wednesday's star midfielder was born over 3000 miles away on the other side of the Atlantic and brought up on a sporting diet of Gridiron and baseball. Hardly someone you would expect to lift the Rumbelows Final at Wembley — but that's exactly what he helped to do last year.

Harkes was a member of the Second Division Sheffield side which defeated Manchester United to win the 1991 Rumbelows League Cup, and put a major trophy in the Wednesday cabinet for the first time in 56 years. And in fact Harkes could have been playing in an Owls shirt even sooner if the United States team hadn't qualified for the World Cup Finals.

But far from having any regrets about taking longer to fulfil his ambition to play in this country, John thinks waiting the extra year actually helped him to get a contract.

He says, "I came over to Britain for trials with Wednesday before the World Cup, but I felt I should be in America preparing with the rest of the squad for Italy. So I returned to America. It worked out well because the kind of exposure the players were given in the Finals we just wouldn't have had anywhere else.

"I am sure being on the television and all the attention we received helped a great deal when the time came for me to look for a club in the U.K. I had trials with Glasgow Celtic and Barnsley before finally settling for Sheffield.

"Wednesday is a great club. I really like it here. And after going to Wembley and winning the League Cup in my first season in English football I know I made the right choice. Some players wait their whole careers for a chance to play at Wembley — I made it in just eight months!

"I know how lucky I've been and I will always remember that day."

The son of Scottish parents, John was born in Kearny, a small town in New Jersey. His first taste of soccer success was as a player in the American international side — the first United States team to reach the World Cup Finals. And although the USA did not qualify for the later rounds of the competition, being there itself was an achievement for a country more used to scoring touchdowns than goals.

"We were thrilled at the thought of going to Italy to play alongside the best in the world," says John. "We were in the same group as Austria, Czechoslovakia and the host nation Italy, so it wasn't really surprising we didn't qualify for the next round.

"But we learned some lessons and hopefully we'll do better in 1994 with the new manager, Bora Milutinovic. I think we'll have a stronger squad, and being in front of our own fans will help."

FIFA's decision to host the 1994 World Cup Finals in America — a country with no outdoor professional league set-up — came in for a lot of criticism, especially from other footballing nations with a fine pedigree of club and national teams. One of the biggest fears is that there is insufficient interest in our brand of football in the States, but Harkes insists this is nonsense.

"It is understandable that some people will not like the idea of a country with no history of soccer holding the sport's greatest event," says Harkes. "But in the 1984 Olympics in Los Angeles soccer was the biggest crowd-puller.

"There were actually 104,000 people at the final, and when the national team plays at home we get crowds of around 40-60,000. The interest in the game is definitely there.

"America certainly has the resources. The stadia are fabulous, and the organisation put into big events like the Olympics and the World Cup is second-to-none, so I have no doubt that U.S.A. '94 will be even better than Italia '90. Hopefully the host nation will even qualify for the second round!" ends John on an optimistic note!

HOLD ON!

Manchester United's Mark Hughes finds an arm-lock helps keep Manchester City's Steve Redmond at close quarters.

EOIN JESS *Aberdeen*

This is the message from CEC PODD, Football Community Officer with Leeds United.

Welcome To

OCTOBER 10, 1988 may go down in the history of Leeds United as a turning point in the club's fortunes on and off the park.

On that date two new faces joined the Elland Road staff. The achievements of Leeds' boss Howard Wilkinson are well known but those of Cec Podd may not be so familiar.

Cec is the 'Football in the Community' officer at Elland Road and is employed by the players' union, The Professional Footballers'

Association. His job is to assist Leeds United to forge links between the club and the local community.

Many would consider such a task to be difficult at Leeds, with the club's reputation for hooliganism among its supporters during the eighties. But Leeds are confident the Community scheme has gone a long way to wiping out the hooligan element and

attracting families back to football.

The scheme was started by former Blackpool and Middlesbrough player Micky Burns in Manchester in 1986. Manchester United led the way before the scheme spread to other Lancashire clubs and then across the Pennines to Yorkshire. This year the

A typical pre-kick-off scene in the Yorkshire Evening Post Family Stand at Elland Road.

Photograph courtesy of Yorkshire Evening

scheme is being introduced to Midlands clubs and it is hoped that all 92 League clubs will soon participate.

Cec Podd sees his duties as an opportunity to put something back into the game after playing more than 500 games for Bradford City.

As Cec explains, "After

them with qualified staff. The stand also has a cafe and games room where the families can watch video highlights of the match on television," Cec goes on.

"I would estimate that 75 per cent of kids have not seen a game at Elland Road because of the fear of hooliganism. The

player along either to coach the pupils or give a talk on what it's like to be a professional footballer. We're aware that players have a great influence over youngsters and we try to incorporate other things in our talks, such as getting homework done and not to talk to strangers.

Elland Road

Bradford City I moved to Scarborough where I damaged a knee. I knew that following the operation my career would effectively be over, so I looked for other avenues in the game to explore.

"The PFA told me that Bradford were setting up a Football in the Community scheme and there was a vacancy as assistant to Eric McManus. I enjoyed the experience there so much that when Leeds started their own scheme I applied for a job. I've lived in Leeds all my life and have contacts here. So I was pleased to accept when the post was offered to me.

"Football in the Community was initiated by the PFA because the players wanted to create a good image. The object is to break down barriers between the clubs and the fans. In the past, fans came to Elland Road only on match days. We want to open the club's doors and make people feel welcome every day of the week. After all, it's really their club," Cec points out.

"The club have built a family stand in the South Stand which was opened at the beginning of the 1990-91 season, and Football in the Community is helping to promote that. We go into schools and various organisations to get families to come along to watch matches.

"There is a creche in the stand so mothers can bring their babies to games and leave

parents won't allow their kids to go to the ground without proper supervision. So we invite a group who have never seen a game to come along as our guests in the Family stand and I'm glad to say that many come back regularly after that.

"We organise tours around Elland Road and they are very popular. We could fill a whole week just showing groups of people around the ground. We encourage it because it lets people see what Leeds is really about and they can appreciate the organisation behind such a big club and how important it is to the city.

"We attract people from all sections of the community. We run tea dances for senior citizens who may not want to come to games because of congestion on match days. We try to get some players to go along to the dances.

"There is also an area designated for the disabled so they can watch the match in comfort. We also do special tours of Elland Road for the disabled and organise coaching sessions for the mentally handicapped. So, just about everyone is catered for at the club.

"Of course, we also look to the future and by liaising with schools we try to attract young people back to Elland Road. We either target schools in certain areas or get phone calls from a school inviting us along. We do coaching sessions and bring a

"For many boys their ambition is to play professional football, so we encourage them to get qualifications, because if they don't have them then clubs — especially Leeds — would send them to college anyway," explains Cec.

"As well as my duties at the club I've also got nine trainees seconded to me as part of Employment Training. I teach them all aspects of my job and with most of them wanting to be coaches they come along to schools and organisations and assist me in coaching sessions.

"We are planning a lunchtime 5-a-side league between companies. We hope to put up a trophy for the winners. A lot of companies will buy a sponsor's box or put an advertising sign up in the ground, so we aim to extend their relationship with the club and give them something back as thanks for their financial support to the club.

"I'm also organising a ladies' football team to represent the club in a league competition. It started with a piece in the programme inviting girls of any age to come along for coaching on Friday nights. We started in September with eight girls and now have over 40 aged between 8-28 years," ends Cec proudly.

So Leeds United and Football in the Community are working hard to end the reputation of Leeds as the troubled club of the Football League.

THE FIVE WISE MEN!

How the pools panel decide who will be a millionaire!

TONY GREEN

ARTHUR ELLIS

GORDON BANKS

ROGER HUNT

RONNIE SIMPSON

FIVE men locked away in a top hotel room, a security guard posted outside the door. Inside a sixth man presides over the meeting. The possible destination of hundreds of thousands of pounds is in the hands of these men!

Sounds like a scene in a best-selling thriller, doesn't it? In fact, the five gentlemen in question, plus their chairman, are the Pools Panel.

They are the men whose forecasts of postponed matches could possibly decide which of the 12 million who do the football pools each week could become a millionaire overnight.

Since the winter of 1963 a panel has been in operation to make their judgement on postponed matches. It was originated because during that winter almost all of the football programme in Britain was wiped out by the weather. The football coupons could not operate. The pools companies had to send back all the stakes to the millions of clients who had a go on the treble chance.

Initially, 31 games had to be cancelled before the panel were called in to deliberate. Gradually down the years it has been reduced until nowadays if only one match has to be postponed then the Pools Panel have to sit.

The current five are made up of former England 1966 World Cup winners Roger Hunt (ex-Liverpool striker) and Gordon Banks (ex-Stoke City goalkeeper), ex-Scottish international and one-time Blackpool and Newcastle midfielder Tony Green, former Celtic and Scotland 'keeper Ronnie Simpson and vice-chairman Arthur Ellis, former international referee and the only surviving member of the panel since '63. They are presided over by chairman Lord Peston, who is the trade and industry spokesman for the Labour Party in the House of Lords.

The six travel to the Hilton Hotel in Park Lane, London every Friday night between the first Saturday in November to the last Saturday in April. A total of 26 weeks.

If no matches are cancelled on the Saturday then they are allowed to go their separate ways.

However, when a match on the coupon is off then the panel meet behind locked doors in a suite in the hotel around two o'clock and a security guard remains outside the door.

Inside, the five-man panel are provided with statistical information — home and away records of the individual sides for the last eight matches — to help them come to their conclusions.

There are no telephones, television, radios or newspapers. They are cut off from the outside world to ensure that nothing can influence their decisions. The panel have no idea of the scores of the games underway.

The five men will discuss the possible outcome of a certain match and then a majority decision is accepted on their verdict. On average about three minutes is needed per deliberation.

At four o'clock, when the playable matches are just entering the second half, their judgements on the postponed games are handed to the chairman and subsequently onto the pools promoters. Then the panel are dismissed until the next Friday night when they'll meet again.

Checking their forecasts against the actual results of matches when they are eventually played is not a completely accurate guide to the success of the Pools Panel. There can be changes in circumstances, form and such like as the weeks or months go by before a rearranged game is played. Nevertheless they are reckoned to get a third of their results correct. And in the unpredictable world of football that's an average that few could better.

BRIAN McCLAIR *Manchester United*

MY MUM KNEW BEST...

...ADMITS CRYSTAL PALACE SHOOTING STAR
IAN WRIGHT

WINNING my first full England international cap last season meant a lot to me. But it meant even more to my mum. She's so proud of me she wears my England cap around the house while she does the housework! I've always handed over my caps and medals to my mum. She's the one who has always had faith in me, and encouraged me to play football.

I never thought I would make it as a professional after being turned down by several clubs as a schoolboy. I reckoned I was destined for a career as a labourer. But my mum always said I was good enough.

Playing for England was a dream come true. It meant so much to win my first cap at Wembley against Cameroon, in front of my family. I know who was the proudest person in the ground — and it wasn't me!

It was great for me to be able to give mum my England cap. I hope there will be plenty of others. I worked so hard to get into the England squad, I'm determined to stay there now.

When I was first called into the seniors last season, I was a bit overawed at being in the company of all the top players. At the team hotel, I was looking round at all the big names as if to say 'what am I doing here?'

But England manager Graham Taylor made me feel at home. He told me I wasn't there to stand around and admire the others. I was there because I was good enough to be selected alongside them.

He gave me the confidence to feel comfortable amongst the England players. By the time I made my debut I was really confident. I felt I was going to score a goal, but that didn't happen.

The one decent chance that did come my way was snapped up by Gary Lineker, who got there a yard ahead of me. That's one thing I learned that night — to keep up with Gary!

He thinks so fast. Following in on shots he was always a yard ahead of me. I made up my mind I would have to make sure I was always level with Gary in the box if we ever played together again.

It would be great to establish as good an understanding for England as I have at club level with Mark Bright. People look on us as a partnership. We work at our understanding. When I'm in a one-on-one situation, Mark knows I will be looking for him in the box. I know instinctively where he is.

Mark is good at holding the ball up, and bringing people into the game. He's strong in the air. My strength is my pace, and the way I can turn players.

We've scored goals together ever since we were first paired up, and I'd love to see Mark get a chance at international level as well.

When we were in mid-table in the Second Division, we both signed new contracts with Crystal Palace because we had confidence in the future of the club, and in our ability to do well. Since then we have been rewarded with new deals. I hope we can go on scoring goals together for Palace.

We've both come from non-League football, so we know what it's like to have to work for a living. We appreciate we're well-off playing football, and are still prepared to work hard to better ourselves.

When we won promotion to the First Division, I knew I would have to sharpen up my game to be able to score goals. I made up my mind to work at it. I figured that Italian football is

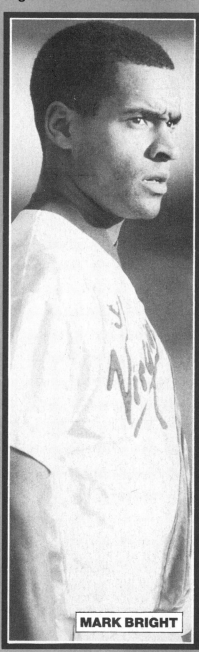

MARK BRIGHT

the toughest there is for strikers. In Italy they get even less time on the ball than we do.

I asked our chairman to supply me with regular videos of Italian club football from satellite TV transmissions. I studied them for hours.

I wanted to learn how the Italian strikers handled the close marking, and tried to add it to my game. There were a few guidelines I picked up, and tried to follow all the time. Such as only taking two touches of the ball in the box before getting off a shot. And never giving the ball away.

In the lower divisions you can get away with taking more time. But in the top flight you have to be a lot sharper, and make the most of any chances that come your way. Everybody thinks quicker at top level. Your reactions have to be that much faster. You have less time on the ball.

Just because I have won an England cap, it doesn't mean I'm satisfied with my game. I want to score more goals. That's the only way a striker is judged.

Of course, scoring goals is not everything. I scored two in the FA Cup Final against Manchester United, but they didn't mean that much because we lost the replay. I would have been happier if I had failed to score — but ended up on the winning side.

Last season Palace made a great challenge to Liverpool and Arsenal at the top of the First Division. I really hope it has established us as one of the top clubs.

Finding ourselves up in the top three early in the season was like finding myself in the international squad. It was a case of trying not to be overawed at being up with the big names. Of believing we were there on merit. We had to show the top clubs respect, but not look up to them too much.

It was great to experience life at the top, having known what it was like at the bottom, the previous year. It's much nicer!

There's not the same pressure. When you're involved in a relegation battle you go out knowing you MUST win three points. When you're at the top, you want to win three points, but the pressure on you is not the same.

Having committed my future to Crystal Palace, I hope to spend much more time at the top in the next few years.

I hope I win some more honours — and so does my mum!

COLIN HENDRY *Manchester City*

CRASH LANDING!

Aston Villa's Ian Olney gets in the tackle that sends Q.P.R.'s Paul Parker heading for a fall!

LURE OF

How money talks

LOTHAR MATTHÄUS
(Inter Milan & Germany)

W ORLD CUP '90 is already a fading memory. Now we are looking forward to the thrills of Sweden '92, and the finals of the European Championships.

The 1994 World Cup is scheduled for the USA, where the public are maybe too hooked on baseball, grid-iron football and basketball to get worked up about soccer.

But the flavour of Italia '90 lingers on in Italy. Top matches there are like watching a re-run of the World Cup.

Almost everyone who was anyone in the World Cup is playing at club level in Italy. Germans, Argentinians, Brazilians, Czechs, Dutchmen — they are all there, along with the occasional Swede, Uruguayan, Hungarian and Russian.

Half of the Germans' World Champion team make their living in Italy — skipper Lothar Matthäus, defenders Andy Brehme and Thomas Berthold, midfield man Thomas Hassler, strikers Jurgen Klinsmann and Rudy Voeller.

Although Maradona departed last season, top striker Claudio Caniggia waves the Argentinian flag in Italy. Strikers Careca, Muller, and Evair, defenders Julio Cesar and Dunga, and midfielders Aldair, Alemao and Mazinho, represent Brazil.

Dutchmen Ruud Gullit, Frank Rijkaard and Marco van Basten made AC Milan invincible in Europe for two seasons, until Marseille toppled them this year.

Tomas Skuhravy celebrated the

offer of a contract with Genoa during the World Cup, by scoring a hat-trick for Czechoslovakia against Costa Rica. He was pipped as leading scorer of Italia '90 only by Schillaci's penalty in the third place play-off against England.

There are top foreign stars in every Italian side. Mikhailichenko (Russia) and Katanec (Czechoslovakia) with Sampdoria; Detar (Hungary) with Bologna; Lacatus (Rumania) with Fiorentina; Brolin (Sweden) and Taffarel (Spain) with Parma; Francescoli (Uruguay) with Cagliari; Martin Vazquez (Spain) with Torino; and Larsen (Denmark) with Pisa.

The attractions are obvious, and one stands out above all others. Cash. Lire. Multi-millions of it.

The Italians pay the highest wages in the world to top players. Anything up to £700,000 a year before bonuses — which can double the income of players with a successful club.

Marco van Basten signed a new contract with Milan before the World Cup, worth £600,000 a year — a little matter of a £150,000 rise! Andy Brehme seems hard done by on only £250,000 a year. But of course he's a defender. Van Basten scores goals — and men who can do that in Italy are worth more than their weight in gold.

Players are treated like superstars. Pampered and flattered, their every need catered for. Luxury treatment is laid on all the way.

Juventus have always had their own training headquarters outside Turin, at Asti. A superb complex with living accommodation and all facilities.

But last year they decided it wasn't good enough for their high-paid stars to spend the night in before matches. So Juventus paid out a total of £200,000 to hire a luxury chateau for one night before each home match.

That sort of cash is small change to many of the club presidents who run the whole show as an expensive hobby. Several are multi-millionaires from business interests.

Juventus is owned by Gianni Agnelli, whose family business is a little car work-shop called Fiat! At Milan, Silvio Berlusconi owns newspapers, T.V. stations and various other big businesses.

New Roma boss Guiseppe Ciarrapico is a leading industrialist known as 'the King of Mineral Water' because he sells more bottles of

THE LIRE
in football-mad Italy

ANDREAS BREHME
(Inter Milan & Germany)

'aqua' than anyone else in Italy.

It's no wonder that Paul Gascoigne has been tempted by the lira-laden offers from Italy. Quite apart from the money, football matches are an event in Italy.

The public are passionate about their football. Their week revolves around the match. The atmosphere is electric. How could it fail to be in the

JURGEN KLINSMANN
(Inter Milan & Germany)

sort of stadia shown to perfection in the World Cup?

When it comes to facilities, the Italians are years ahead. In monetary terms they are about £500 million in advance of British grounds!

When Italy was awarded the 1990 World Cup Finals, the Government passed a special bill authorising the payment of 460 billion lire to the twelve different local authorities who were staging matches. Translated into sterling, that's about £230 million.

The cash was for renovating and upgrading ten of the grounds — and for building two completely new stadiums. And the Italians reckoned that by the time work was completed on all the grounds, costs had doubled.

The Olympic Stadium in Rome was totally rebuilt at an orginal cost of £28 million. A third 'tier' was added to the old San Siro Stadium, and the ground revamped, at a cost of £24 million.

Turin's brand new ground was first priced at £22 million, and the magnificently designed new stadium in Bari was costed at £27 million.

None of the twelve World Cup grounds had less than £10 million spent on them. As far as the Italians are concerned, it was money well spent.

The stadiums looked magnificent to the world-wide audience, and the superb facilities remain for the domestic supporter. Every spectator seated, and most under cover. Plentiful bars, restaurants and toilets.

Families are encouraged. A big match is a carnival occasion. Everyone wears their Sunday-best. Football is the number one interest for the average Italian.

They might have to pay a lot for tickets — £10 perhaps for the cheapest seat — but it is their main form of entertainment. And what entertainment!

More than 50 world-class foreign international stars are currently sparkling in Italy. In eleven years since the borders were re-opened to overseas players, the imports have scored over 1500 goals.

The success of the foreigners persuaded the Italians to lift the permitted limit from three to four imports per club this season.

Milan's rebuilt stadium hosts German stars Matthäus, Brehme and Klinsmann one week, and the Dutch trio of Gullit, Rijkaard and van Basten the next. Plus half the current Italian side one week or the other. 80,000 crowds are common at the big club games.

The Italians are not afraid to lead the way. From the start of the 1993-94 season, all referees handling first and second division matches in Italy will be full professionals.

Before the World Cup they took the historic decision to insist that referees become full-timers. Top whistlers have to make up their minds whether to accept the challenge — or make way for those who will. Leading referees will earn up to £50,000 a year.

Style is important to Italians. They like things to be perfect. Amateur refs in charge of multi-million pound players didn't seem right.

They appreciate style on the pitch. Roberto Baggio, Italy's equivalent to Paul Gascoigne, is hero-worshipped in Italy. They love players with flair and imagination.

English football may be tougher and more demanding. The Football League Championship may be just as hard to win as the Italian.

But until proposed plans for a British 'Super-League' come to reality, for the star-struck football fan Italy is the place to be.

Shadowed

Sheffield United's TONY AGANA finds GARY PALLISTER (Manchester United) keeping a closer than close watch on him.

PAUL STEWART
Tottenham Hotspur

ALEX FERGUSON

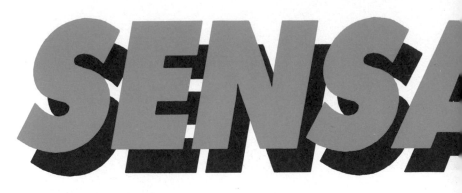

OCTOBER

Nineteen-year-old Lee (signed from Torquay for £85,000) was being used sparingly by United as he got used to the harsher life of the First Division. At this stage, he perhaps did not have the physical strength needed for the top flight, but he was already impressing the critics with his blistering pace and ball control.

NOVEMBER

Sharpe almost single-handedly destroyed Arsenal's Rumbelows Cup challenge with a dazzling display in front of a 41,000 crowd at Highbury. He scored a hat-trick in the 6-2 humiliation of the eventual League Champions. He showed his enjoyment of the feat by demonstrating the famous 'Sharpie samba' in the corner of the pitch, delighting the travelling fans but annoying manager Alex Ferguson.

DECEMBER

Sharpe continued his scoring streak with the only goal against Everton and once again he did his dance at the corner flag. But this time his manager told him, in no uncertain terms, to cut it out!

JANUARY

Lee showed his ability to provide as well as score goals when he linked superbly with Mark Hughes to put Third Division Bolton out of the FA Cup. United had looked nervous until Sharpe provided the cross for Hughes to hammer a volley into the Wanderers net.

FEBRUARY

Alex Ferguson blasted Rumbelows Cup semi-final opponents Leeds for their treatment of Lee during the first leg at Old Trafford. Said Fergie, "The lad was kicked from pillar to post, and he still scored a goal. Young Sharpe answered all the questions about his ability today. Teams now go out to stop him. He's a marked man."

Lee, however, had the last laugh when he made sure of a Manchester Wembley date. He scored in the second leg to put the trophy beyond the reach of the Elland Road side. Showing great coolness, he latched on to a through ball from Brian McClair and rounded keeper Lukic, before slamming in the goal from an almost impossible angle.

After the match, though, Lee was left to wonder whether or not he'd be on the receiving end of a fine from his manager. As his team-mates celebrated his winner, he did his samba dance, after being told not to by Fergie.

He defended himself saying, "I couldn't help celebrating today. It was a spur of the moment thing. I felt so good."

Unfortunately, things did not go as well for Manchester United in the other Cup competition. Their hopes of retaining the trophy were dashed as their Carrow Road jinx continued when they crashed out of the FA Cup to Norwich.

Lee didn't have one of his best games. He missed an easy shot on the edge of the box, and the Manchester outfit lost 2-1.

MARCH

Lee was voted the PFA's Young Player Of The Year at a ceremony in London (it was a double for United as Mark Hughes was given the Player Of The Year award). Lee was then pulled out of the England Under-21 squad at the eleventh hour and moved into the senior squad for the crucial European Championship match against the Republic of Ireland at Wembley.

He said, "It has all happened so quickly I can hardly believe it. I have just signed a new five-year contract with United and I was looking at about two years before I was pushing for a place in the England squad. But I have surprised myself this season. I was really expecting to be in and out of the side."

Lee made a second-half appearance, replacing Arsenal skipper Tony Adams and becoming the youngest player for eight years to pull on an England jersey. His impact was such that manager Graham Taylor admitted he might have been wrong in not playing the youngster from the start.

"Having got the taste, I think I can cope at senior international level," said Lee.

APRIL

A busy month for the Manchester United winger. He took a big step towards becoming the youngest millionaire in football by signing an endorsement deal with boot firm Asics worth £100,000. The sponsorship will run right through to the 1994 World Cup Finals in the United States.

It was the biggest contract ever offered to a teenage soccer player in Britain, and was a big bonus for Sharpe, coming hot on the heels of his international debut and new £500,000 five-year contract with his club.

The lad the players call 'Roadrunner' then travelled to Poland for United's Cup Winners' Cup semi-final first leg clash against Legia Warsaw. Sharpe's amazing pace played a key part in the English club's 3-1 win. He overwhelmed the Legia full-backs with his speed and skill. Eventually it paid off when he was held back by defender Marek Jozwiak while running for goal. Jozwiak was sent off and the Poles never recovered from the killer blow.

Next was the Rumbelows League Cup Final against Sheffield Wednesday at Wembley. However, it was obvious Wednesday boss Ron Atkinson

TIONAL!

A super season for Manchester United's rising star LEE SHARPE

had done his homework on who the Manchester danger man was. Despite some early promise, the young winger was effectively marked out of the game by the combined efforts of Wednesday's Roland Nilsson and John Harkes. And unfortunately for Lee, United lost 1-0.

MAY

Lee's outstanding season continued as he picked up yet another award — the Barclay's League Young Eagle Of The Year. However, on a negative note, he sustained a calf strain and was forced to pull out of the England squad to face Turkey.

Lee then took part in his greatest triumph of all to date. He was in the Manchester United team which beat Barcelona 2-1 in the final of the European Cup Winners' Cup in Rotterdam. While Mark Hughes scored both United goals, Sharpe thrived on the service he was given from captain Bryan Robson, and kept the opposition defence on its toes with his wide running. When United received their first European trophy since 1968, the smile on Sharpe's face showed what he thought of it all! Only 19 and a European cup final winner's medal in his possession — where does Lee Sharpe go from here?

NIGEL WINTERBURN
(Arsenal)

OLD FIRM RIVALS

Celtic's PETER GRANT and Rangers' MARK HATELEY, show the determination and will-to-win that have made clashes between their clubs such memorable matches.

REPUBLIC of Ireland star Paul McGrath kicked off Aston Villa's new season armed with a new two-year contract — two years after believing that he would have been forced to hang up his boots by now.

Though he is just approaching his 32nd birthday, the former Manchester United star went through a period earlier in his career when a series of knee injuries convinced him that he would have to retire prematurely.

Even at the time of his £450,000 transfer from Old Trafford to Villa Park back in the summer of 1989, there were doubters aplenty who believed the Midlands club were taking a huge gamble.

Since then, however, Paul has not only enhanced his reputation as an accomplished defender-cum-midfield player, but by following a strictly laid down training routine, designed to protect those suspect knees, he now feels he can look forward to at least another five years at the top.

Says Paul, "There was a point during my final few months with Manchester United when I thought I'd be lucky to stretch my career to the age of 32. Knee injuries limited my appearances over my last couple of years with the club.

"But the move to Villa has worked out extremely well from that point of view. I missed only a handful of matches during my opening two seasons here.

"The secret has been that I'm allowed to take an extra day off training whenever I feel it necessary. Instead of being out with the other lads, I go to the gym to work on the weights machine.

"The idea is to build up the muscles around the knees in order to protect them. I lift weights for 15 minutes before every training session anyway, to minimise possible damage, but perhaps one day a week I'll opt for a good, long session rather than normal training.

"I'm sure this routine has prolonged my career. I feel I can play on for as long as anyone else. I'm pretty stiff the day after games so I take things easy and it's OK the following day."

Paul goes on, "I'm delighted with the way things have gone since changing clubs. But I was only able to do it through the help of everybody at Villa. In fact, you would be hard pressed to find a better bunch of lads than those at the club.

"Everyone mixes well and there is a tremendous spirit. We just want to get out on to the pitch and do well for each other.

"To be honest, I was surprised

IT'S ALL CHANGE

for Aston Villa's PAUL McGRATH

by how quickly I was accepted by the players and the fans. I arrived with all sorts of fears about how I would be received.

"It would have been easy for them to look at a player arriving from what is deemed a bigger club and decide, 'He thinks he is stepping down to a lower level.' That being the case, they'd certainly have found it hard to accept me.

"I never felt that way about Villa, though. From the moment I found out they wanted me, I saw it as a chance to join one of the biggest clubs in the country . . . one with a proud history of honours and the potential to win more. If I hadn't seen them in that light, I wouldn't have come in the first place.

"Fortunately, nobody ever doubted the way I felt about Aston Villa. The players welcomed me as a member of the squad from day one and the fans were right behind me as soon as I took to the field wearing a Villa jersey."

Around Old Trafford, McGrath's transfer was seen as the welcome departure of a player who had become a liability.

Off the field problems had damaged his image and helped ruin his Manchester United career. After joining Villa, however, Paul put that side of his life behind him.

He admits, "I was my own worst enemy. My whole outlook on life was completely wrong. I was out simply to enjoy myself. I went through life thinking that everything should be fun, and I certainly went out of my way to enjoy life both inside and outside the game.

"Unfortunately, that meant I wasn't giving football the serious attention it deserved. I learned a lot of lessons. But they eventually sunk in and I no longer regard football as 'just a game'. I have a much more professional approach to my career.

"More importantly, I've learned to treat other people seriously, especially those who are important to me.

"My move from Manchester United was the starting point. Since joining Aston Villa, I've matured a lot.

"During the past couple of years, I've been more responsible and got on with playing football for Aston Villa."

PAUL McGRATH —
looking forward to a new season and renewing his partnership with former manager Ron Atkinson.

KENNY SANSOM
(Coventry City)

EDGED OUT!

Sheffield United's PAUL BEESLEY has to look sharp to blot out the challenge of ace striker LEE CHAPMAN (Leeds United).

ANDY WALKER

IT'S BEEN

admits Celtic striker
TOMMY COYNE

IT would be a slight under-statement to say my career with Celtic has had a few ups and downs.

In the last two and a bit years I've experienced the joy of signing for my boyhood favourites, the agony of losing my place in the first team and then being put on the open-to-transfer list, and the relief of finally winning my place back and finishing top goalscorer in the Premier League.

The First of March 1989 will always stick in my memory. It was the day I moved from Dundee to Celtic, my heroes as a youngster.

After breaking through in season 1981-82 with Clydebank, then moving to Dundee United and then Dundee, I felt I learnt my trade thoroughly.

I think scoring 37 goals in season 1987-88 with Dundee persuaded Celtic to pay £500,000 for my services. It was a move most players only dream of, but, 15 months later, I experienced an all-time low when I was put on the transfer list.

By the start of last season I was out of things so much I didn't even appear in the team group photo. Talk about being out of the picture!

It all came as a shock to me. After gradually building up my career I felt everything was fitting into place with one of the biggest clubs in the land, but I was then left on the first team sidelines and playing only second string football.

But even when things aren't going your way, you've always got to believe your situation will change at some point. Every player must have a positive approach — even when things aren't going to plan.

With my name on the transfer list there was nothing I could do except get my head down, carry on playing and hope the breaks would come my way.

A ROLLER-COASTER!

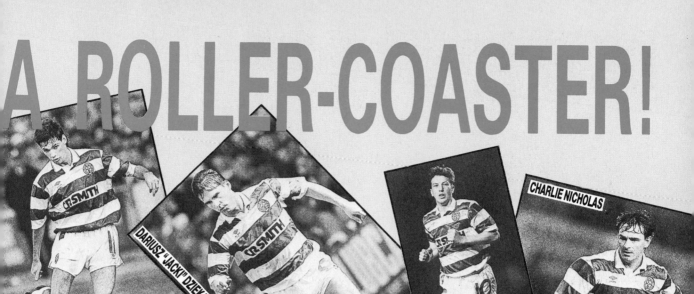

DARIUSZ "JACKI" DZIEKANOWSKI

JOE MILLER

CHARLIE NICHOLAS

GERRY CREANEY

I scored 10 goals in about 12 reserve games at the start of last term so at least something was going right for me.

And my confidence in my own ability never dropped at any point, either. The reserve team staff, Benny Rooney and Bobby Lennox, gave me a lot of encouragement at the time and I appreciate everything they did for me.

As well as that, because I was on the transfer list at the time, there was an incentive for me to do well because someone from another club may have been watching. I never went out with the attitude that I wasn't going to try. I still had a lot to prove.

Thankfully my misery came to an end when I was called back into the first team in November for a midweek League game with Motherwell at Parkhead.

I had been drafted in partly because of mounting injury problems and partly due to the lack of goals the team had been scoring. Thankfully, I managed to score both our goals in our 2-1 win and my whole future seemed to change immediately.

Scoring twice in my first game back definitely gave me the boost I needed. But I've always felt that, given a regular game, I'll score goals for any team I play for.

I admit I hadn't scored that often for Celtic immediately after my move from Dundee, but I think the manager was trying different permutations with his strikers and that affected my own performances.

Besides myself, there was at one time or another, Mark McGhee, Frank McAvennie, Andy Walker, Joe Miller, Gerry Creaney, Dariusz Dziekanowski and Charlie Nicholas to choose from.

But everything seemed to change after that Motherwell game. I reverted to being a first team regular once again, and by finishing last season with 19 goals to my credit I'd like to think I didn't let myself or the team down.

It's just unfortunate that the team hasn't won a trophy in the last two seasons. We have had more than our fair share of problems in recent years. But I honestly believed that everything was going to change in 1991.

After a shaky start to last season we began to get into our stride after Christmas and we enjoyed a long unbeaten run.

We were out of the League race by that time, so we were relying on the Scottish Cup as a means of picking up some silverware and qualifying for Europe once again.

Our crunch game came in the quarter-finals when we were drawn against Old Firm rivals Rangers. They had already won the Skol Cup and were well ahead in the Premier Division, so the treble was definitely on the cards for them.

On the day, however, they had three players sent off and we went on to win 2-0. Celtic have always had a proud history in the Cup and we all felt it was going to be our year in that competition.

However, Motherwell put paid to any thoughts of green and white ribbons on the famous old trophy when they beat us 4-2 in the semi-final replay at Hampden. It was one of the worst experiences of my life and one I don't want to repeat.

Nevertheless, we still managed to take something out of such a disappointing time. We pipped Dundee United for third place in the Premier League on the final day of last season which qualified us for the UEFA Cup.

After missing out on Europe last year it was vital for a club of Celtic's stature to face the top continental sides once again.

Hopefully, the good times are just around the corner at Celtic Park. Every player at Parkhead is determined to put events of the last two years to the back of their minds and look forward to the future.

FOOTBALL DAFT!

. . . and
Jack Murray has
the evidence to prove it!

AS Jack Murray knows, philately will get you everywhere — and when it comes to football, he's got it licked!

For the amiable Glaswegian is acknowledged as having one of the best collections of football stamps and commemorative memorabilia in the world.

Jack was recently awarded the Gold Medal for the Court of Honour exhibition in China — recognition for building up a 75 volume collection, dating back to the last century.

His life's work includes volumes on Scottish, European, Olympic and World Cup football, as well as an A-Z of Foreign Nations and four volumes of 'meeting the stars'.

Jack explained how this hobby began;

"I started collecting stamps at the age of ten, but after fifteen I concentrated on football, because it was what I knew the most about.

One of my best buys was the first-ever set of stamps issued to commemorate a football tournament — on a specially prepared envelope with a Victory postmark — for the 1924 Olympics in Paris, when Uruguay won the gold. I bought

them for £30 forty years ago, but they'd be worth a four figure sum now.

"My collection is what it is because of one thing — I'm football daft. The most important thing about collecting is knowing your subject. I've managed to pick up some rare stamps and postcards just through my knowledge of football.

"For example, I once picked up a franked envelope bearing the date of the first ever international between Scotland and England, 30th November 1872. I got it for 10p, for the value of the stamp alone. What had been overlooked was the importance of the date it was issued.

"On another occasion, I found a postcard of the Racing Club, Paris, dated 1900 — the year Paris hosted the second modern Olympic Games. It cost 75p! I've also obtained the only known postcard commemorating the first World Cup, in Uruguay in 1930."

Jack communicates with philatelists world wide, and bids in international auctions.

"I was fortunate enough to be invited to Spain for the World Cup in 1982, as the British representative in a group of twelve judged to have the best collections in the world. Needless to say, I had the time of my life! Between the twelve of us, we put on a tremendous exhibition.

"Each of us had an outstanding piece in our collection. Mine was a set of stamps from the 1966 World Cup, which had been printed with colours missing, making them very rare indeed — and fairly valuable.

"I'd been at the World Cup in 1986, and was lucky enough to be given a ticket for the 1990 final. The only condition was that Italy had to be playing in it, so when Argentina's replacement 'keeper, Goycochea, saved the penalties from Donadoni and Serena in the semi-final, that was my trip scuppered!

"At the moment, I'm preparing exhibitions for Porto and Barcelona. I've already displayed all over the world, from San Marino to South Korea.

"I think it's a shame that we don't have a football museum in Britain — after all, who invented the game?"

Over the years, Jack has met many of the game's great names — and he rates Ferenc Puskas as one of the gents of the sport.

"I first met Puskas in 1960, after he'd played in one of the greatest games ever seen — when Real Madrid beat Eintracht Frankfurt 7-3 in front of 135,000 people at Hampden Park in Glasgow.

"He's a marvellous man, and I've met him several times since that occasion.

"I first met Pele in 1966 when Scotland played Brazil, and I was glad to see him back again for the Under-16's World Cup in 1990. Generally, I've always found players to be approachable and helpful, when they find out my hobby."

When Jack proudly displays his two special Celtic albums, which he compiled to celebrate the 100th anniversary of the club in 1988, you might think his personal favourites are the Parkhead giants.

But it's with Partick Thistle, the First Division club which is so often the butt of jokes, that Jack's allegiance lies.

"I'd have to delve back in time to recall Thistle's last moment of glory, in 1971 when they defeated Celtic in the League Cup Final. One of my prize possessions is a postcard, signed by that Thistle team and franked for that very day. I've managed to persuade my son, Stephen, into supporting the Jags, but unfortunately he's not the least bit interested in continuing my collection!"

JACK MURRAY WITH THE GREAT PELE

G LYN HODGES' transfer to Sheffield United last season hinged on the income from a Grand National Sweepstake!

That was the bizarre situation the on-loan midfielder from Crystal Palace found himself in when the hard-up Bramall Lane club couldn't afford the £400,000 asking price.

So keen were the Blades to sign the Welsh international permanently that the money raised from their lottery on the famous horse race went towards the Hodges transfer fund . . . and Glyn himself was so eager to make the switch from Palace to Sheffield United that he even bought tickets himself.

Thus, the 28-year-old found himself in the unique position of helping to pay for his own transfer!

"It was a nice feeling to know that the fans really wanted me at the club," recalls Glyn. "The fact they were prepared to put their hands in their pockets in order to buy me was a remarkable gesture.

"Even more amazing was the fact that they didn't mind that I'd snubbed the chance to join United nine months earlier! Then I'd decided to move to Crystal Palace instead of coming to Bramall Lane when I left Watford last summer.

"The fact the fans were coughing up their own hard-earned cash in order to land me did put me under a bit of pressure. I had to try to put it to the back of my mind. If I hadn't, it might have affected my game and then they wouldn't have wanted to buy me!"

It all worked out well though. The Grand National sweepstake was a success and enough money was scraped together to pay Crystal Palace their fee.

It was the chance to team up with Sheffield United boss Dave Bassett for the third time — he served under him at Wimbledon and Watford — that persuaded Hodges at the second time of asking to have another go at settling down at a northern club.

Apart from a three-month unsuccessful spell with Newcastle United, Glyn had spent all his football career close to his London birthplace.

Hodges knew straightaway that football fans in the north were a different breed to those he'd been used to in the capital. That was confirmed by their eagerness to contribute towards

HE HELPED PAY HIS OWN TRANSFER FEE!

The story behind GLYN HODGES' move to Sheffield United.

his transfer.

"Football is a very important way of life in this part of the country. I didn't realise how fanatical supporters could be," Hodges goes on.

"In Sheffield you see people walking around the steets during the week wearing club scarves and tracksuits, not just on match days. I never saw that in London.

"Here everybody knows you are a footballer. You are recognised on the steets or whenever you go out. They want to talk football to you all the time. That suits me because I can talk for hours about the game!

"Being recognised is a new thing for me. London is so vast that you can go out and nobody knows who you are. Sometimes even your neighbours don't know you are a footballer.

"I enjoy being in a more football-orientated city."

RICHARD SHAW *Crystal Palace*

RAY HOUGHTON
Liverpool

DAVID PLATT *Aston Villa*

SET-BACK PUT ME ON THE RIGHT ROAD!

Arsenal 'keeper **DAVID SEAMAN** explains why.

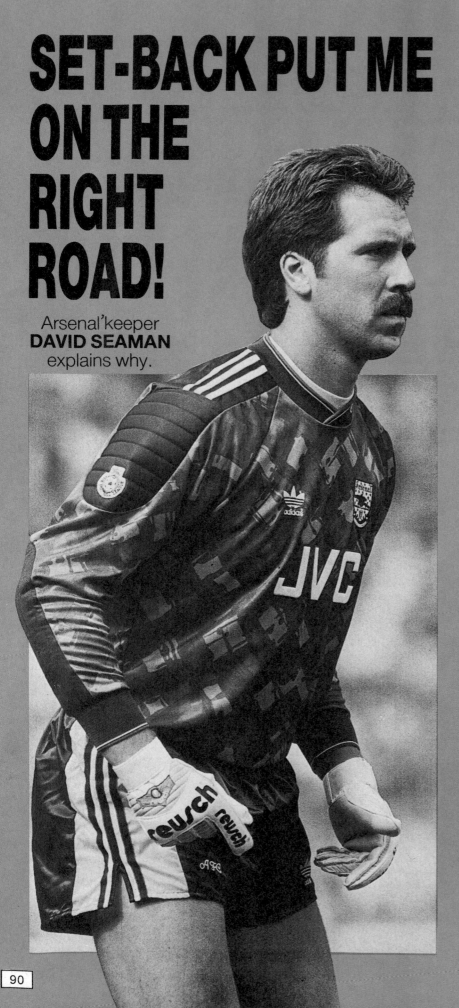

WINNING the Barclays League title last season was the happiest moment of my life — and I believe it was all set up for me by the unhappiest moment nearly nine years before.

I was 19 at the time. A reserve goalkeeper with Leeds United. We were newly relegated from the First Division, with Eddie Gray as new manager in place of Allan Clarke.

Ahead of me for the first team place was a certain John Lukic. I thought I was ready to challenge him. But the manager told me that because John was only 21, and I was 19, he wanted more experience for the goalkeeping position — and he couldn't afford to keep both of us.

The manager said he was letting me go. I was very upset. I didn't know what to do. Leeds were the only team I wanted to play for. I'd been a supporter all my life (and I still am a fan). I thought my goalkeeping career was over, that I would never be good enough to play at top level.

Eddie said he hoped I would get a chance somewhere else, but I couldn't see much chance of that. Within a few days, however, I was fixed up. Martin Wilkinson, who had been assistant manager at Leeds, was in charge at Peterborough United. He heard I was available and got in touch.

I went down to Peterborough, signed for the club, and I've never looked back since.

I went straight into the first team and got the kind of League experience I'd never have got in the reserves at Leeds. It turned out to be the best thing that could have happened.

Playing for Peterborough was a real eye-opener for me. When you're with a top club you don't get any idea of what goes on in the lower divisions.

I had it in my head that it was only in the First Division that people took the game seriously. I somehow thought they played for fun lower down the League!

It really surprised me that everything at Peterborough was just as serious as it was at

Leeds. You had to be just as professional in the Fourth Division as in the First. Perhaps more so because everything was done on a shoe-string budget.

I learned a lot in two years at Peterborough, getting tremendous help from physio Bill Harvey. But then came another big moment in my career — a transfer to Birmingham City.

Manager Ron Saunders had sold Tony Coton to Watford, and bought me to replace him. Ron Saunders was to become one of the biggest influences on my career. He had been a very successful striker as a player, but he seemed to know more about goalkeeping than any 'keeper. Perhaps that's why he scored so many goals — he knew exactly what the goalkeeper didn't like!

Ron took the goalkeepers for specialist training at Birmingham, and taught me a lot. It was a great experience. We won promotion the first season, and although we dropped back down the next, I enjoyed it.

After two years I moved on again, to Queen's Park Rangers. Another step up the ladder, and another major influence on me, in goalkeeper coach Bob Wilson.

Bob has taken me in training ever since, at both Rangers and Arsenal. He's very thorough in examining the technical side of goalkeeping.

We use videos to analyse my performances, and work on weaknesses. We look at every mistake and try to learn from it. But the great thing about Bob is that we spend more time watching my good saves than my errors.

It's a matter of confidence. We analyse the mistakes, but we don't dwell too much on them. Bob would rather I remember the great saves, to boost my confidence.

If you start thinking about the mistakes too much, you are likely to make another one. You are better off thinking about the good saves and the clean sheets.

In training, Bob won't let me finish a session until I've made a great save. We carry on until I've got one last great save to keep in my mind, and boost my confidence.

Last season was a fantastic one for me. I start every year with the aim of keeping as many clean sheets as possible, but even I didn't dare hope for as many as 24 in the First Division and 29 in all matches.

At one time we hoped to beat Liverpool's incredible record of conceding only 16 goals in a full season, but in the end we just missed it.

Being really self-critical, I could have got that record if I had not messed up on two goals. I mis-punched a ball, and let in a soft goal against Wimbledon. And I let in a near-post header against Everton that I should have prevented.

Of course, there were those FA Cup semi-final goals at Wembley when we lost to Spurs. That was a bad day for me.

I feel I should have saved Gazza's free-kick. My studs seemed to catch in the ground as I moved to the shot. I didn't get the lift I needed, and only got my finger-tips to it. And I definitely should have saved Gary Lineker's second goal.

Having watched them on video, I just put those errors out of my mind. I accept there are going to be occasional days like that. The main thing is to limit them to the minimum.

I know in myself that my training is right. I can't do anything more. Mistakes don't affect my confidence. I just remember the good games.

I will look back on the games at Liverpool and Spurs, and on my save from Gary McAllister in the first FA Cup-tie against Leeds. I can't do much better than in those performances.

I don't believe I actually was a better goalkeeper last season than in the past couple of years. It was just a matter of gaining in confidence.

It was a boost for me to join a club like Arsenal. They seem to do everything right. They make me feel proud to be playing for them.

It took a long time to get the transfer sorted out. My old pal John Lukic was the man in possession, and I didn't want to tread on his toes — but once Arsenal had made their move for me, I was determined to sign for them.

Everything lived up to expectations. Greater atmosphere at home games, more exposure in the papers, more televised matches.

I hoped the move would lead to greater involvement with England, and that's just what happened. Halfway through the season I won the place from Chris Woods.

With due respect to QPR, I don't know if that would have happened if I had still been at Loftus Road, even if I did make my international debut as a Rangers player. Now I hope to establish myself as England goalkeeper for the next few years.

I had a taste of the World Cup atmosphere in Italy before going home with an injury. Now I want to be there for the next big tournament.

When I went to Italy, I knew I wouldn't really be in contention for a place in the team. Peter Shilton and Chris Woods were the recognised first and second choice. So damaging my thumb, and being forced to go home, was not such a big disappointment as it might have been.

Next time I hope to be the number one, but that means continuing to do well for the Arsenal. The only way to get noticed is to do well for your club — and the bigger the club, the better.

You can't get any bigger, or better, than the Arsenal. That early set-back from Leeds was a real blessing in disguise.

JOHN LUKIC

MIKE NEWELL *Everton*

I Surrender!

Wimbledon's JOHN FASHANU gives in to the pressure of Nottingham Forest's GARRY PARKER.

FRESH START FOR
THE BIG MAN!

WHEN Manchester City boss Howard Kendall shelled out £750,000 to sign Niall Quinn from Arsenal in March 1990, the lanky striker was worried he wouldn't live up to the price tag . . . he needn't have worried!

Kendall rescued the marksman from three years in the Football Combination with Arsenal Reserves and breathed new life into a career which started full of promise at Highbury and then showed signs of fizzling out.

Quinn vowed to repay the faith shown in him by City, and a look at his achievements at Maine Road indicates that the move has proved to be a boost for the player, and a bargain deal for the club.

His goals following his move to City helped ensure the club's survival in the First Division in season 1989-90. Last season he was the club's leading scorer and established himself as Eire's top striker after a couple of years on the international sidelines while struggling at Arsenal.

So regular first-team football at Manchester City has helped dispel the detractors who claim that Quinn's only asset is his aerial prowess.

The height factor is still important, but there is now a fair measure of skill on display as well.

"I can't think of anything nicer people could say about me," Niall confesses. "I'm very pleased when folk point out my touch has improved. I've worked hard on it.

"Some people still remember me as a very raw player who spent six seasons at Arsenal but played only 50-odd games. It would be fair to say that in those days I was purely a big target man.

"I feel I have much more to offer these days. I feel comfortable with the ball at my feet. I'm not just a big target man to whom people sling high balls.

"Sometimes I feel the fact that being tall has worked against me. Folk believe that all a tall player can do is head a ball.

"But, thankfully, City fans have learned not to expect me to be a player who possesses all the skills. What they have seen is an

The move that gave Manchester City's NIALL QUINN a new lease of life.

honest, whole-hearted trier who has more to offer than some believe.

"My aim is to do as well as Graeme Sharp has done for Everton. He's what I aspire to be. Graeme has the two main aspects of the job down to a fine art. He is a superb target man who also scores great goals.

"I'm not a natural scorer like, say, Gary Lineker, but my scoring record isn't bad. I have to work really hard to get into scoring positions. It's coming. But I'm certainly not going to get worried about it.

"Indeed, I'm not too anxious to be suddenly thought of as a scorer. I've never set targets and won't do so now. It's ridiculous to look at players in terms of facts and figures.

"For example, my partner at City for most of last season, Adrian Heath, struggled as far as goals were concerned. Yet he gets through an amazing amount of work and is easy to play alongside.

"His running has given me opportunities to get into the box to finish off moves, boosting my total, possibly at the expense of his.

"I'm certainly not getting carried away by my goals record. I won't allow myself to look for goals at the expense of my target man duties, for instance.

"When Howard Kendall spent all that money on me he wasn't buying a goalscorer. Let's face it, he wouldn't have bought me on the strength of only a few goals at Highbury.

"What is more important than

being amongst the goals is the fact that, for the first time in many seasons, I've been able to play regular first-team football. After three years playing reserve football, I've had a run of about 50 games in 12 months and find that I'm now getting into the swing of things."

Last season proved to be the most rewarding season the Irish striker has had in his career, not just at club level, but at international level as well.

At one stage, he had netted six goals in nine international starts and was such a threat that England boss Graham Taylor altered his team formation for both England and Eire European Championship clashes last season simply to counter him.

But Quinn admits that he is not an automatic choice for an Eire side which vied with England for a place in the European Championship finals in Sweden next summer.

He continues, "Eire boss Jack Charlton does things his way. He selects players to do certain jobs irrespective of what's happening at club level. So I know that, despite my regular outings in a City team which is doing well, plus being a regular in the side for over a year, nothing is guaranteed.

"The important thing is that when I link up with Ireland nowadays I know I have a chance of making the starting eleven. That wasn't the case before I joined Manchester City and started playing regular first-team football," he ends.

GRAEME SHARP

MEL STERLAND *Leeds United*

GARY STEVENS
Rangers

IT was the proudest moment of my career when I led out the West Ham side for the match that clinched promotion to the First Division last season.

It was disappointing to miss out on the Second Division Championship at the last gasp. Oldham's final minute penalty—winner snatched the title from us on the last day, but there was still tremendous pride for me in captaining the team.

Until last season I had never skippered any team at any level. Being asked to take over, when Julian Dicks was injured, was a huge boost to my confidence — even if it was a big surprise.

I was on the treatment table, getting an ankle strapped before a game, when coach Ronnie Boyce came over. I wondered what I'd done wrong.

But he just said 'Skipper?'. I said 'Yeah, love to', but I didn't expect to keep the job for more than one game. To lead the team to promotion was something special.

I really don't know why I was given the job. There are several other players at Upton Park with more experience, and more years of service to the club.

Whatever the reasons, I loved it. I always like keeping busy, being involved in everything on the field. I hate matches when things seem to have passed me by.

I knew Julian Dicks was likely to reclaim the captain's role when he was fit again, but I did enjoy standing in. It has done a lot for my confidence.

Last season was a wonderful time. It was great to win promotion for the people I rate the best fans in the country. I get a real thrill from the atmosphere at Upton Park.

I will never forget the encouragement they gave us when we lost in the FA Cup semi-final at Villa Park. Anyone would have thought we had won the cup the way our fans supported us. After that demonstration of loyalty, we just had to clinch a promotion place.

The EastEnders remind me of home — in Liverpool. They are genuine people like the Scousers. I feel very settled at West Ham.

Strangely, as a kid I was an Arsenal fan. Liam Brady was my hero. I never dreamed I would get the chance to play in the same side as him. But when I joined West Ham, Liam was in his last season in the game. It was a privilege to play and train with him.

I never told him I was a big fan of his. But at the end of his final game, he gave me his shirt — and it's now one of my prize possessions.

I will never be the same kind of player as Liam. I wouldn't claim to be in the same class. He's the best I ever played with, and I would love to think a little of his ability rubbed off on me. I'm sure I gained a lot from watching him play and train.

I'm very conscious of the great tradition of midfield players at West Ham — stars like Martin Peters, Trevor Brooking, Alan Devonshire and Liam. It's a lot to live up to, but they are all different types of player, and I have to develop my own style.

I like to be creative. I don't like giving the ball away, but I accept I could be more dominant, and a better ball winner.

When I joined Everton from school, I never liked to pass the ball at all. But they cured me of that. In training if anyone had more than two touches, coach Colin Harvey would shout 'get rid of the ball' — and then crash into you from behind.

But he was a big influence on me, and I still have a lot of respect for him. Sadly, things didn't work out for me at Everton.

My first-team career lasted just

20 minutes — as a substitute! That was only due to so many injuries amongst the squad. I was normally about sixth in line for a place.

And I remember so little about my debut — against Manchester United — the match video is the only proof I've got that I actually played!

I went on loan to Crewe, and was then sold to Carlisle. There I had mixed fortunes. We won promotion one season, and went straight back down a year later. The next season we finished second bottom of the Fourth Division.

TO BE A MMER

IAN BISHOP
West Ham's midfielder says his piece.

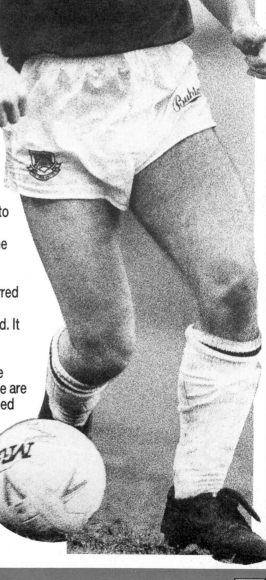

I missed five months of the season with a mystery ankle injury. I heard a 'crack' in the joint, but nobody ever pin-pointed the trouble. It was some kind of ligament damage.

It wouldn't clear up, and I got really down. Towards the end of the season, with my contract running out, I became desperate. Against doctor's orders I started playing again to try to attract some interest from other clubs.

I thought the injury had wrecked my chances of a move up the scale. But to my surprise, Bournemouth came in with an offer, and I went down to the south coast.

It was my first taste of the West Ham style. Manager Harry Redknapp was a confirmed Hammers man and passed on all the good habits from Upton Park.

I've since discovered the atmosphere at Bournemouth was actually very similar to West Ham. They play the game the right way, and get enjoyment from it.

Harry gave me back my enthusiasm, and I really enjoyed myself at Dean Court, before moving on again to Manchester City.

There I was doing well, until the arrival of Howard Kendall — my old Everton boss — as manager. He didn't rate me as a player, and certainly didn't appreciate my long hair. He was always telling me to get it cut — and once he cut it himself, after I'd come out of the shower!

However, it was still disappointing when he transferred Trevor Morley and me to West Ham in exchange for Mark Ward. It meant I was dropping down a division once again.

But I couldn't be happier the way things have worked out. We are back in the First Division; I earned a call-up at the end of last season to the England B squad; and manager Billy Bonds is happy to let me grow my hair long!

Now I hope to build on last season's success with West Ham and on the international scene.

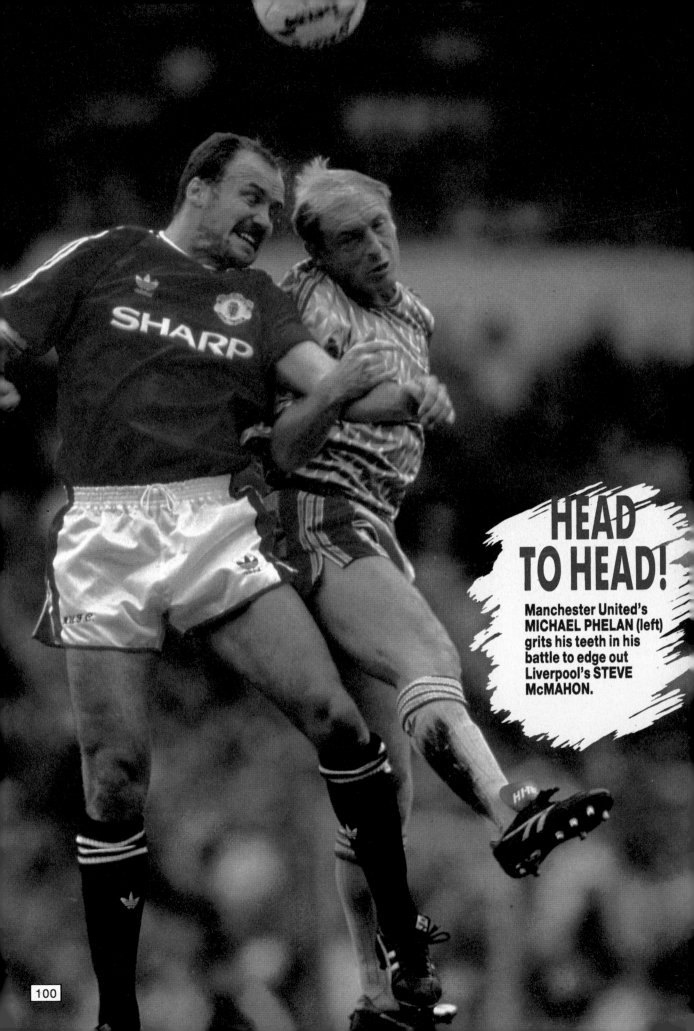

HEAD TO HEAD!

Manchester United's **MICHAEL PHELAN** (left) grits his teeth in his battle to edge out Liverpool's **STEVE McMAHON**.

NICK HENRY
(Oldham)

EARL BARRETT captained Oldham Athletic to the Second Division Championship last season and a return to the First Division after an absence of 68 years. His outstanding performances in the heart of the Oldham defence caught the eye of England boss Graham Taylor and led to a call-up to the full England squad which toured Australia, New Zealand and Malaysia last summer.

Not bad for a 24-year-old who failed to gain a regular first-team slot at Manchester City and was the subject of a bargain £35,000 transfer to Oldham in November, 1987 after just four appearances for the Maine Road club.

Earl explains, "I failed to break into the City team because other players had established themselves as first-team regulars. I realised that I was either in for a long wait before getting my chance or I would have to move to another club. I took the latter option and it paid off for me.

"City didn't put any pressure on me to leave. They were prepared to let me stay and fight my way into the side, so we parted on friendly terms. I didn't mind leaving Maine Road but it was the thought of leaving all my friends behind that was the hardest to accept.

"In those days Oldham's finances were not as good as they are now and the club worked with a small squad of players. Oldham wanted me on loan, but decided to sign me when they were hit by injury. I started off playing left-back when our regular in that position, Andy Barlow, was injured."

Earl continues, "In that first term we struggled in the Second Division but improved a lot over the course of the next three seasons. In season 1989-90 we reached the Littlewoods Cup Final before losing to Nottingham Forest, and the FA Cup semi-final in which we were beaten by Manchester United. We went close to promotion to the First Division, just missing out on a play-off place.

"Naturally, it was a big

Oldham star
EARL BARRETT
explains why.

disappointment but we were determined to make up for it last season and, thankfully, everything came good in the end.

"During my time at Oldham I've played at full-back, centre-half, midfield and striker so I have been something of a utility player. But last season I played regularly at centre-half. Having a settled position helped my overall performance.

"I was given the Oldham captaincy early last season and that came as a big surprise to me," Earl goes on. "I wasn't first choice for the job. When Mike Milligan left to go to Everton, Andy Holden was handed the captaincy and when he was injured it was passed to Andy Ritchie. Andy also fell victim to injury and I was next in line to be captain. I've held it ever since.

"When I was with Manchester City I never really stood up for myself in team matters. For instance, I wouldn't go into the manager's officer and ask why he had dropped me. I would keep my feelings to myself. That's not really the type captains are made from. But I've come a long way since then and now have the confidence to give advice to other players. I'm still a very quiet man but I know that I've got to do a lot of shouting on the park and try to motivate the players.

"From the opening matches of last season I could sense it was going to be our year. There was a buzz about the town. Crowds were about 4000 up on the previous season as the fans sensed we had a squad capable of making it this time.

"We got the perfect start to our League campaign when we went 16 matches without defeat, opening up a large gap over the clubs in the play-off positions. We had a big first-team squad which meant that when we picked up injuries there were players able to come in and fill the position.

"For instance, we had four quality strikers in Andy Ritchie, Roger Palmer, Ian Marshall and David Currie and all played their part in scoring crucial goals. They were all injured at some stage so

having other options was very important. Certainly if Andy and Ian had been fit for the whole season we would have been promoted earlier than we were.

"Another player who played a large part in our success was Richard Jobson. The previous season we had a habit of giving away stupid goals. That was solved when we bought Richard from Hull City at the beginning of last season. He partnered me in central defence and that took a lot of pressure off me.

"Before he arrived I had to mark the big target men and I have to admit it was a difficult job. Although Richard is not a big man he can outjump most opponents and that left me just having to pick up the pieces.

"In previous seasons we've been accused of not being good battlers. But last term we fought all the way and won many of our matches with late goals because we showed stamina and determination other teams couldn't match.

"We were close to promotion for about a month before we actually clinched it. It was a marvellous feeling when we went to Portman Road on April 27 and won 2-1 to take us up. We took nearly 5000 fans to Ipswich and the scenes at the full-time whistle will live with me for a long time.

"There is no secret way to gain success. It's a mixture of ability and hard work. It does help though to be with a friendly club. I enjoyed my time at Manchester City, but they do have some strict rules, which isn't the case at Oldham. Boundary Park is very relaxed from the boss down to the cleaners. If someone steps out of line Mr Royle will let them know. But he doesn't bear any grudges and is welcoming to everyone.

"There are no stars in the Oldham side, just hard-working professionals. Anyway, if any of us do get too big for our boots we'd have to contend with dressing room funnyman Rick Holden. He brings everyone down to earth with a few practical jokes and some good-natured insults.

"However, we do have a star man . . . and that is Mr Royle. If anyone deserved promotion it was the boss. He has been manager here for 10 years and when he took over, the club were going nowhere.

"He has pulled us around and taken us to the First Division for the first time in 68 years. He turned down the chance of going to a bigger club and that shows his loyalty to Oldham.

"We aim to repay that by giving him a First Division team to be proud of," Earl ends.

JOE ROYLE

103

JOHN COLLINS
(Celtic)

JUST CHAMPION!

Arsenal's LEE DIXON shows what it feels like when your team has topped the league!

Chris Fairclough

WHEN Leeds United bounced back into the big-time last season, manager Howard Wilkinson had prepared his team for the struggle promoted clubs often face.

He had added £2.5 million of talent to an already experienced team which, at that time, included the likes of Gordon Strachan, Lee Chapman, Mel Sterland and Chris Fairclough.

John Lukic, Gary McAllister and Chris Whyte were the men recruited by Wilkinson to boost Leeds. But while they certainly did the business during the Elland Road side's first campaign back in the top flight, one other player who really caught the eye was youngster David Batty.

It was to be the 21-year-old's first taste of Division One. But while many expected him to make a slow start and glean knowledge of how to get by from the older and wiser men in the team, the locally-born midfielder had other ideas right from the off.

"I knew I would benefit enormously from playing alongside the likes of Gordon and Gary. They know what it's all about. I knew their presence would help me when I was in the thick of the action but I thought I could help them, too," explains David.

"That's how it was when we won the Second Division Championship. It was achieved through a complete team effort. We helped each other. But as far

AN AFTERNOON NAP HELPED SORT ME OUT!

Leeds midfield dynamo DAVID BATTY explains

Chris Whyte

Gary McAllister

as preparing for my initial season in Division One was concerned, I avoided going round the rest of the lads asking what I should expect.

"I wanted to find out for myself. That's what I've been doing since former manager Billy Bremner made me captain of the club's youth team. There is no substitute for learning from your own experience.

"The season we were promoted from Division Two was the best I had had, even though I was dropped in April and had to settle for a place on the substitutes' bench for the last few games.

"I believe there were two reasons why I dropped out of the final team. Firstly there was tiredness. I'd played in all of our first forty games that year and probably wasn't strong enough at that time to cope with many more. The manager noticed this and that's when he left me out.

"I decided I was feeling tired during games because I wasn't having enough rest during the week. After training in the morning I'd go out and do something in the afternoons.

"I had never been one for sleeping during the day, but I disciplined myself to go to bed for a couple of hours after training. Once I had started to do that I began to feel fresher and sharper," David continues.

"The other reason the boss left me out was my lack of goals, something I wanted to improve on in the First Division but didn't.

"During our Second Division promotion season the manager wanted to step up the goal count from midfield. That meant changes and since I hadn't scored all season I was the obvious choice to stand down.

"Goalscoring has always been my downfall, yet I don't believe it's through failing to get into scoring positions. I'm always hovering around the penalty area when we're on the attack.

"Last season I started to work on my shooting in training. But I failed to score again last term. Goalscoring is certainly one part of my game I would like to improve.

"As for my stamina, I have always been convinced that would take care of itself. I'm stronger now than I was during our promotion season and I've filled out a bit as a natural part of growing up."

David found growing up in the First Division quite easy as well. The difference in his stature stood him in good stead as he received full England squad recognition last term.

His first call-up came for England's European Championship match against the Republic of Ireland in Dublin in November 1990. He then found himself involved in the international scene more or less all the way through the remainder of the season.

But in a typically unselfish manner the Yorshire lad is quick to point out the influence of his club boss Howard Wilkinson.

"Until he took over as manager of Leeds my disciplinary record was poor," admits David. "I was regularly getting into trouble with referees as well as missing quite a few matches through suspensions.

"I was labelled quick-tempered but I maintain my problems were due to inexperience. Mr Wilkinson has drummed into me the senselessness of continually falling foul of officials. It's bad enough having to miss games through injury, but having to sit them out because you are suspended is totally irresponsible. I have learned that lesson."

If he keeps on learning as quickly, it looks as though David Batty could be a well-known name in world soccer before very long.

GORDON COWANS
Aston Villa

FAMILY FUN!

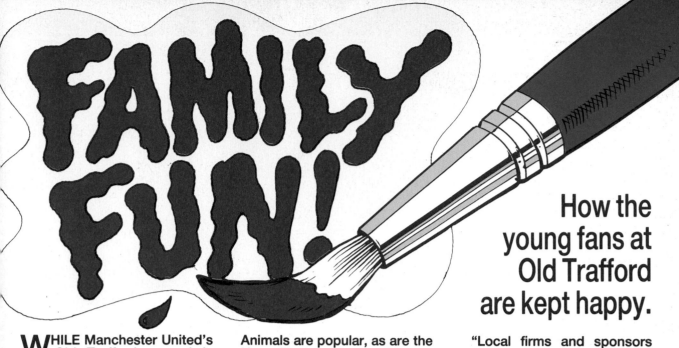

How the young fans at Old Trafford are kept happy.

WHILE Manchester United's Old Trafford ground is usually full by 3 o'clock on match days a certain part of the showpiece ground is packed to the rafters a full two hours before that.

The family stand has room for 2000 people but before a game it has to cope with quite a few more who aren't there to see the football. Those extras are at Old Trafford to entertain the kids before kick-off.

"Face painting is a very popular entertainment," says Barry Moorhouse, the man in charge of family affairs at the ground. "We vary the entertainments from match to match but the face painters make several trips here over a season.

"The kids want to be made up in all kinds of disguises. Animals are popular, as are the Hero Turtles along with our very own club mascot — the Red Devil. Unfortunately each face takes two or three minutes to do so we can't get through all the children who want their faces done.

"The queues are usually very big and we can only manage 50 or 60 kids in a day. But there are a lot of other entertainments put on to keep the families amused. We have comedians, clowns and balloon modellers and all of them are very popular.

"We have a stage erected and our guests perform there. There are some weeks, however, when we don't have entertainers but instead run a family disco before the game.

"The match-day host in the family stand, 'Uncle Dave', also arranges for players from the junior teams and the first-team to come up before the game to sign autographs for the youngsters.

"Local firms and sponsors are also very generous in donating free gifts and souvenirs for everyone. The sponsors of the Football League, Barclays Bank, are one such firm. We also give out soccer magazines and chocolate bars plus stickers and sticker albums.

"The souvenir shop here at Old Trafford also donates gifts such as Manchester United pens and posters. Everything we give to the kids is appreciated.

"The family stand here is always the first area of the ground to sell out. We would very much like to extend it," ends Barry.

It would also be a good idea to look for a few more face painters!

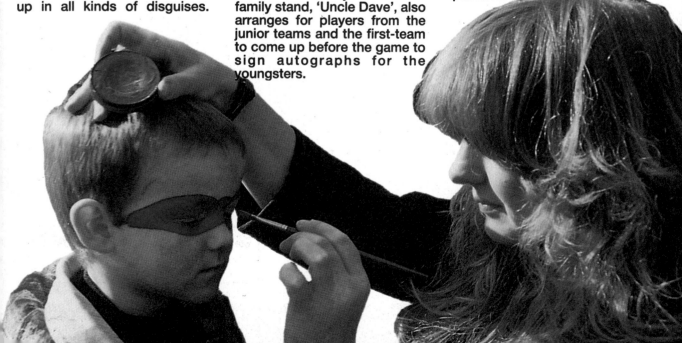

FIG

HTING BACK

— that's Rangers' IAN DURRANT

I ENDED two-and-a-half years of misery by returning to the Rangers' first-team near the end of last season. I played a part in the 2-0 victory over Aberdeen which brought the Premier Division title to Ibrox on the final day.

But, as I attempt to fully re-establish myself as a first-team regular this term, I'd like all Rangers fans to forget about my performances and just concentrate on supporting the team.

When I made my return last season, I was on a high for the first few games. But now I'm just another guy battling for a place. And I want the supporters to regard me in that light.

Yet, along with my family and everyone at the club, they have been absolutely fantastic during my recovery from the knee ligament damage sustained at Pittodrie in October, 1988.

They've supported me through thick and thin and I'll never forget their backing in the reserve match against Hibs last season in which I started my second comeback.

So many people turned up to cheer me on that the club had to open up the Copland Road stand as the Govan one was full. Normally, the Govan is the only stand in operation for reserve matches, so you can appreciate how overwhelmed I was.

But, contrary to popular belief, I haven't had any problems coping with the pressure generated by having to live up to people's expectations on my return.

When you've been out of action for as long as I was, folk tend to remember all the good things you did and forget all the bad things. Therefore, they think of you as a better player than you actually were.

But everyone has been very supportive and I don't feel they have made things difficult for me at all.

I've learned that returning from major injuries is all about guts and determination and I think I have shown plenty of both.

But I know I still have a lot of work to do if I am to fulfil my potential.

I feel much better this term for having gone through pre-season training during the summer.

I hadn't had pre-season training for two years due to the injury and, when I came back last term, the lack of it had a drastic effect on my overall standard fitness.

I was playing matches last season when I was only 70 per cent fit. As a result, I was dead on my feet over the last twenty minutes of a game.

Pre-season training builds you up both mentally and physically and I do feel I have benefitted tremendously from it.

However, being stuck on the sidelines with the injury did, believe it or not, have some long-term benefits for me.

Three years ago, my tackling was suspect. But, these days, I feel I am stronger and more capable of mixing it a bit.

During my comeback, I had to work with weights and do circuit training before I could actually begin running again. And, due to the type of work and exercise I was doing, I put on about ten pounds in muscle weight.

When I returned to the side last season, I re-assured everyone that I wouldn't be shirking tackles. And, believe me, that is still the case.

If I did begin entering challenges in a half-hearted fashion, I wouldn't be doing my job properly. Initially, I was a little reluctant to put 100% effort into tackles as I wasn't entirely sure of how my knee would react. But I realised it

was simply a matter of confidence and I'm now going in where it hurts at every possible opportunity.

There was a lot of sympathy shown for me from various quarters when I was out through injury. But I don't expect anyone to give me an easier time on the field because of that.

My knee does feel different than it did before. This is because, when I was over in America last year, I had an Achilles' tendon implanted where my damaged medial ligament was.

But the movement of my knee is in no way restricted and I feel no worry about stretching it if necessary.

The operation in America was a massive success, due in no small part to the advanced technology over there.

That was the second time my knee had been operated on. I tried to make a comeback in February of 1989. But, after playing in a handful of reserve matches, I broke down again.

That attempt to get back into action was very much make-or-break and, unfortunately, it didn't work out.

There was still a bit of movement in my knee at that point in time and, in retrospect, I realise it probably wasn't right. It was swelling up after every game and giving me a lot of problems. I knew within myself that there was every chance I'd have to be operated on again.

It's due to setbacks of that nature that I owe a massive debt to the boss, Walter Smith, and the now-departed Graeme Souness for the faith they showed in me during my lay-off.

And I would really love to repay them by stringing together a run of consistent performances this season.

But, as I've pointed out, a lot of people have spent time and effort getting my career back on the rails. And that has to be paid back.

BARRY HORNE
(Southampton)

JOHN BARNES *Liverpool*

FRANCE OR

Southampton's
MATTHEW LE TISSIER
had a big decision to make

MATTHEW LE TISSIER'S goal-scoring exploits have put Guernsey on the football map. Before he burst on to the scene at Southampton, few people expected a top-class player to be found there.

The Channel Islands have no professional leagues, so not many English scouts go there to spot the local talent. Le Tissier was an exception.

After making his debut for the Saints as a 17-year-old, it wasn't too long before he was being asked to decide about his international future. Did he want to play for England, where he played his football or did he want to turn instead to France, where his family had originally come from?

For a while, Le Tissier was very interested in plying his skills for the exciting French team. But former England manager, Bobby Robson, put a stop to such thoughts by calling him up for an England Under-20 tour to Brazil and then an England B game.

That game against Eire B wasn't the most auspicious of starts to an international career for Le Tissier.

"The game was played at Cork in very windy conditions on a bumpy pitch," Matt now recalls. "Not the ideal setting to make a good impression on your international debut for the B team.

"I was given only the first-half of the match to prove myself and that wasn't easy. To make matters worse the team lost 4-1 and I didn't feel too good after that."

Despite the disappointment of that match in Cork, Le Tissier had proved that a lad from the Channel Islands could make it to the top in the game.

"I suppose I was lucky to be spotted by Southampton because not many people are aware of football in Guernsey. Scouts from the mainland are rare visitors and that's a shame because there are some very talented players over there," Matthew points out.

"I think there are still plenty of lads on the islands just dreaming of the chance to play for a Football League club. It would be great to see a few more of my fellow islanders in England.

"The big game every year in the Channel Islands is the challenge match between Jersey and Guernsey. It was a game I played in myself as a youngster with current Chelsea player, Graeme Le Saux, amongst the opposition.

"Not long after that I travelled to the mainland with Graeme to sign YTS forms with Southampton. The Dell was the obvious destination for any promising young islanders because Southampton's where the ferries go to.

"Graeme didn't make it at Southampton but he was to be given another chance with Chelsea where last season he began to show what a very good player he will be.

"It wasn't easy for me to make the break-through either. Although I made my League debut back in 1986 when I was still 17, it took me another three years before I could be sure of a first-team place.

"During that time I was involved in 20 odd games a season, with plenty more as sub, but I just couldn't keep hold of my shirt on a regular basis. My big problem was inconsistency — I'd turn it on in one game and be useless in the next."

The turning point finally came when Danny Wallace departed for Manchester United, leaving Matt to form a striking-partnership with Danny's younger brother Rodney.

"I just couldn't get in to the team because of the Wallace brothers but when Danny left the club, former manager Chris Nicholl gave us our chance," explains Matthew.

"The boss's philosophy was always to play attacking football and that couldn't have suited Rodney and myself better. We were both given free-roles and we did our best to make the most of them.

"Ours was not a normal sort of striking partnership. We didn't play in set positions as with a big target-man and a smaller quick man.

"Our understanding worked on instinct. We were on the same wavelength and always seemed to know what the other would do at any stage during the match.

"A goalscoring partnership is not something you can really practise. It depends on whether you hit it off together. You either know about each other's play, or you don't.

"By the end of that first season together Rod and I had scored 45 goals between us in League and Cup matches.

"All in all that was an exceptional season for me and I loved every minute of it. But I knew that it wouldn't be as easy after that especially when Rod signed for Leeds."

The rewards for such a brilliant season came quickly for Le Tissier. He beat Aston Villa's Tony Daley and his friend, Rodney Wallace, to win the Professional Footballers Association 'Young Player of the Year' award and also won the 'Barclays Young Eagle of the Year' trophy, as well as the Southampton 'Player of the Year' vote.

After collecting the PFA award, Matthew slipped home early with Wallace to make sure they were in good shape for training the next day at Southampton. He'd kept the whole thing quiet from his team-mates, who didn't know

ENGLAND?

a thing about it until they read it in the newspapers the next day!

After all that success, it seemed a foregone conclusion that Matthew would make his full international debut for England last season. But having missed out on an England B trip to Algeria through illness, he was not called on again throughout what was an inconsistent and injury-plagued season, despite the fact he still ended up with 23 League and Cup goals.

Missing the Algeria game led to some suggestions that Matthew hadn't made the effort to join up with the England squad in the heavy snow conditions at the time. But he was quick to dismiss any thoughts that he might not want to play for England.

"I was astonished that there was such a fuss made about the whole thing. To suggest I didn't want to go to Algeria was nonsense. I'd set my heart on playing for England but I had the 'flu so there was nothing I could do about it.

"There were times last season when I took a bit of stick for my performances," admits Matthew. "But the only way I know to stop the knockers is to keep putting the ball in the back of the net."

Le Tissier has the individual skill to match the likes of Paul Gascoigne — but staying at Southampton allowed him to avoid the sort of attention that Gazza attracted all last season.

"I don't know how anybody could cope with that sort of pressure all the time," says Matthew. "Personally I just want to concentrate on my football and that's why I've been more than happy to start my career with a club like Southampton.

"If I had moved to a big club too early in my career I would not have been happy with all the Press coverage that would have come with it. They tend to build you up only to knock you down when something goes wrong.

"No, I'm quite happy to leave all the fuss to others as long as one day I will be playing regularly in the England team," ends Matthew.

SUPER FAN

That's a title that's been well-earned by far-travelled MARTIN FONE

JUST who are the best fans in Great Britain — supporters of the likes of Celtic, Rangers or Manchester United who follow their respective teams in thousands?

What about Scotland's Tartan Army who travel the miles to see their country in action?

Or how about the handful of fans who follow lower division or non-League clubs year after year, with very little chance of ever seeing their heroes win any kind of trophy?

Alternatively, there is always the Super Fan who keeps up with football all over the world, often visiting the most far-flung places.

That's where many people's vote would go, and in particular to the likes of Shrewsbury Town fanatic Martin Fone. Ever since the age of 11, Martin has kept a close eye on the game around the globe.

Now, at 36, he can boast seeing games in no fewer than twelve different countries and three Continents.

"My father took me to my first game back in 1966," Martin remembers. "It was between Shrewsbury Town and Bournemouth. At that time I relied on my dad to take me to matches. I started going regularly by myself at about the age of 14.

"A year or so later I took my first away trip. That was in 1970 when I went to the Baseball Ground in Derby to watch Shrewsbury play a Cup-tie. Derby were a good First Division team at that time and had Brian Clough as manager.

"It wasn't until I was 16 or so that I began to travel regularly.

"Then things really got going when I went to study at Cambridge University. Watching Shrewsbury meant I could combine seeing my favourite team and going home to Shropshire.

"I also started to go to every away game during my time at Cambridge, and I also visited most of the grounds in the east of England such as Ipswich, Norwich and Colchester.

"Shrewsbury had a pretty eventful time of it in the seventies and eighties and I saw them progress from the Fourth Division to the Second," says Martin. "Doing this I visited most of the English grounds without really keeping a tally.

"When it became obvious to me that I had only a handful of grounds left to visit I began to make a conscious effort to reach them. I was living in London at the time and had friends who were trying to do the same thing. I got to my 92nd ground in 1981 — it was Anfield, home of Liverpool.

"I had waited for Shrewsbury to be drawn away there in one of the cup competitions. The years went by without them meeting. It was then I realised that Liverpool were obviously frightened of the Shrews!

"So I made the journey to Merseyside to watch a League Cup-tie against Swindon.

"Ironically, the ground of Liverpool's neighbours Everton, Goodison Park, is my favourite English stadium. I think it's mainly due to the magnificent three-tiered main stand.

"I've also visited all the grounds in Scotland and that's where you can find my favourite British arena — Rangers' Ibrox Park."

But Martin hasn't confined his ground-hopping to the United Kingdom. His travels have also taken him abroad — to Europe, South America and Australia.

"I spent some time working in Australia and managed to see four National League games there. A couple of friends and myself also took twelve days in Chile to see the South American Championships last summer.

"We also journeyed to Italy to watch the 1990 World Cup. That's where I saw my most spectacular stadiums. But in addition to this I have visited every ground in the German Bundesliga, all but one in Holland, half of those in the French First Division as well as some in Austria, East Germany and Belgium.

"There isn't that much of a language barrier when we travel abroad. Going to other countries you learn the important phrases. It's also a help that the locals seem to speak at least some English. That's quite embarrassing really. If a German were to ask directions in his own language in this country, it would be unlikely anyone would be able to help. That isn't the case in Europe where many people speak our language."

One kindly Belgian steward spoke Martin's native tongue and ended up driving him and his friends forty miles to a Fourth Division game.

"We were at a game in Kortrijk and learnt there were two Division Four matches kicking off an hour and a half after the end of our match," explains Martin. "We picked one out in a small town and then discovered there was no public transport to it.

"So we decided to visit the other town Menen. We asked the steward if he knew how we could get there and he offered to take us in his car. On the way, though, we learnt that he, in fact, lived in the town we had originally wanted to visit!

"We usually see all these grounds in two-week periods when we go to a particular country and pick up a two-week rail pass. There are still a lot of places I would like to go, particularly other countries in eastern Europe.

"As for my favourite ground abroad I have to say it belongs to the German Bundesliga club Bochum. I am also fond of the Olympic Stadium in Munich, but that becomes one of my least favourite venues when it rains."

Even super fans can't laugh off the weather.

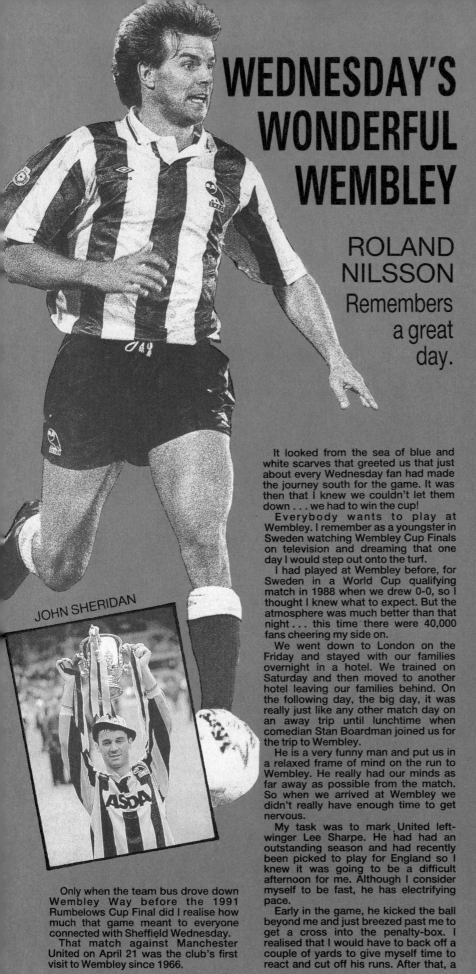

JOHN SHERIDAN

WEDNESDAY'S WONDERFUL WEMBLEY

ROLAND NILSSON Remembers a great day.

Only when the team bus drove down Wembley Way before the 1991 Rumbelows Cup Final did I realise how much that game meant to everyone connected with Sheffield Wednesday.

That match against Manchester United on April 21 was the club's first visit to Wembley since 1966.

It looked from the sea of blue and white scarves that greeted us that just about every Wednesday fan had made the journey south for the game. It was then that I knew we couldn't let them down . . . we had to win the cup!

Everybody wants to play at Wembley. I remember as a youngster in Sweden watching Wembley Cup Finals on television and dreaming that one day I would step out onto the turf.

I had played at Wembley before, for Sweden in a World Cup qualifying match in 1988 when we drew 0-0, so I thought I knew what to expect. But the atmosphere was much better than that night . . . this time there were 40,000 fans cheering my side on.

We went down to London on the Friday and stayed with our families overnight in a hotel. We trained on Saturday and then moved to another hotel leaving our families behind. On the following day, the big day, it was really just like any other match day on an away trip until lunchtime when comedian Stan Boardman joined us for the trip to Wembley.

He is a very funny man and put us in a relaxed frame of mind on the run to Wembley. He really had our minds as far away as possible from the match. So when we arrived at Wembley we didn't really have enough time to get nervous.

My task was to mark United left-winger Lee Sharpe. He had had an outstanding season and had recently been picked to play for England so I knew it was going to be a difficult afternoon for me. Although I consider myself to be fast, he has electrifying pace.

Early in the game, he kicked the ball beyond me and just breezed past me to get a cross into the penalty-box. I realised that I would have to back off a couple of yards to give myself time to react and cut off his runs. After that, a few long balls were played over the top of our defence for Lee to use his pace, but I was able to get back before him and clear the danger.

I was pleased with my performance in defence, but I like to get forward where possible and found that I didn't get much opportunity to do so at Wembley. I knew that if I went upfield and we lost possession I would struggle to get back in time to do my marking job on Lee Sharpe.

Apart from that, the Wembley pitch is big and tiring on the legs. When I played at Wembley for Sweden, I learned that too much running around there can lead to players getting cramp. I didn't want that happening to me, so I was careful not to use up all my energy and stamina before the end.

United were the favourites, but that acted as a spur for us to prove we were capable of beating the top sides in the country. It was obvious that the United fans were expecting their side to win, whereas our fans were hopeful, and weren't putting the same pressure on us as United fans put on their team.

There was little to choose between the sides early on, but we gradually took control and deserved our goal when John Sheridan scored in 37 minutes. That boosted us and after that United began to struggle a bit. They were anxious to get back on level terms and began leaving gaps in their defence. We created one or two chances to extend our lead while remaining strong in defence.

It was a great relief when the final whistle went and we could savour the experience of being the first Wednesday side to win a major cup final at Wembley in 56 years.

It was a moment to remember walking up the steps that led to the royal box to receive my winners' medal — one I'll never forget. It was also great to know that my wife and daughter were in the stand to share the experience with me.

It was fitting that our captain Nigel Pearson should lift the cup because he deserved his 'Man of the Match' award for an outstanding defensive performance. He is a great motivator and was able to inspire myself and all the other Wednesday players.

That night we had a party in the hotel with our families and close friends and when we arrived back in Sheffield the following day the reception was tremendous. Thousands of fans were there to welcome us home.

It was part of a great end of season for me after I missed five months through injury. I suffered torn knee ligaments against Millwall at the end of October. Specialists said that it would probably take six or seven months to heal. That meant me missing the rest of the season, so a Wembley trip in April was never really in my plans even when Wednesday were reaching the latter stages of the competition.

It really made up for all the disappointment and frustration when I returned to the side on April 6 against Portsmouth, was able to play in the Cup Final, and then take part in the remaining League games which clinched promotion for us to Division One.

Yes, April 21 was a truly great day for me . . . and season 1990-91 a memorable one!

STUART SLATER *(West Ham)*

ASK any football fan which is the oldest soccer ground in the country and it's likely your reply will come in the shape of a blank stare. Then tell them that this particular stadium is also the oldest in the WORLD and they'll be completely flummoxed.

Even the answer may stump them. After all, how many supporters know that it's the Drill Field, home of G.M. Vauxhall Conference side Nantwich Victoria and that the Vics have been playing there since 1875?

That's when the football and rugby players of the local hare and hounds clubs decided to concentrate solely on Association Football and find new premises. They moved to a nearby regimental drill field and named themselves Victoria after the reigning monarch of the time.

"A few of the club officials were army captains so there was a military influence," says Northwich club president and author of the official club history, Ken Edwards.

"But nobody even thought the Drill Field could have been the oldest ground in the world that has been in continuous use by the same senior club. We qualify as a senior club because we were founder members of the Second Division in 1892.

"It was a remark by the grand old man of Cheshire football, Ted Case, that first gave us the clue. He said that he thought the site may be the oldest and a few other

knowledgeable people agreed with him.

"But there were a few other old grounds that made the same claim, so I decided to research the information. Stoke City had played at the Victoria Ground for a long time, but they didn't start there until 1878. Dumbarton were another club who couldn't beat our record there, while other stadiums hadn't been in continuous use."

The Drill Field now boasts a fine cantilevered concrete and steel grandstand which helps boost the capacity to just under 10,000. But before this was built in 1968, there was an old timber stand.

"Originally on the Dane bank side of the ground near to the River Dane," Ken Edwards continues, "it was put up in the early part of this century. But around the time of World War One it was decided to move it to the other side of the pitch — the site of the present stand.

"It was actually moved across the pitch on a set of rollers. I don't think we'd do that today.

"Unfortunately there is nothing around the ground to tell people we are the oldest in the world, nor do we have any souvenirs to sell. This is partly because we haven't known about the record for long and partly because the Drill Field's future is in doubt.

"When Northwich were in serious financial trouble a few years ago, a firm of land developers bailed-out the club. But in return they were given an option to build on the site if they decided they wanted to.

"Fortunately, they haven't as yet and everyone at the club is hoping they don't before the option expires in May 1992. If we survive then we'll erect a brass plaque, something to tell visitors about the place."

That will mean the end of football's best-kept secret.

THE OLD AND THE NEW!

Two football grounds — but with so different stories to tell!

IN September 1896, Walsall F.C. played host to Glossop North End in a friendly match at their new Hilary Street ground. That stadium, later to be renamed Fellows Park after the club chairman H.L. Fellows, was to become the club's home for the next 94 years.

In 1990 the Saddlers moved house. The Fellows Park site, just a couple of minutes from the busy M6 motorway, had been sold to developers. The plan would bring in £4.5 million of much-needed cash which, in turn, would help banish Walsall's financial worries and provide them with a new ground.

Plans were drawn up for a new stadium to be built on the site of an old sewage works in the Bescot area of the town. Four million pounds and a lot of hard work later the club were ready to open their brand new Bescot Stadium.

But even the name of the new concrete and steel structure wasn't easily come by. The club decided that the supporters should have a say in this and so invited suggestions.

The fact that it had once been used for treating sewage wasn't lost on some witty fans. W.C. Fields was one suggestion received by the club, Flushing Meadows was another. But Bescot Stadium was judged the most suitable and competitive football began there with a 2-2 draw in the Fourth Division against Torquay United.

Despite the presence of 30 or so metal stanchions around the ground there is no contest as to which is the better footballing area, Fellows Park or Bescot Stadium.

With 100 years of football ground history to look back on, and a century of mistakes made to learn from, the ground designers were able to produce a stadium tailor made for football.

Its 12,000 capacity is mostly made up of seats with the two ends behind the goals accommodating standing supporters.

Fans need not just turn up at the ground in time for kick-off, however. They can park their car in any one of 1200 car parking spaces available at the ground before enjoying a meal in the 350-seater restaurant.

Alternatively, for fans wishing to leave the car at home, they can always arrive at the ground by train and its very own Bescot Stadium railway station.

With the implementation of the Taylor report imminent Walsall don't have many worries. The stadium is fireproof because of its concrete and steel structure, and has all the necessary safety precautions in case of crushing.

It will also be possible to rid the ground of its stanchions and make Bescot Stadium cantilevered if that's what the board decides.

Walsall's current Fourth Division status would suggest that won't be necessary in the very near future, but it still doesn't detract from the arena's potential

As secretary Roy Wally says, "Bescot Stadium has to be the most modern ground in the country."

A tough baptism for Queen's

THERE was a crisis last season for Queen's Park Rangers when both their top international defenders — Paul Parker and Alan McDonald — were out with long-term injuries. Replacements were needed in a hurry.

The search for the two men required, took the QPR scouts to Blundell Park and Edgar Street, the homes of unfashionable Grimsby Town and Hereford United respectively.

At Blundell Park they found Andy Tillson and at Edgar Street, Darren Peacock — two players who had never performed at any higher level than the Third Division.

Soon after arriving at Loftus Road, the two players were thrown in at the deep end of Rangers' relegation struggle. They made their League debuts alongside each other on December 23, 1990 against Derby County.

"With the team in such a dangerous position near the foot of the table, we didn't have much time to get used to Division One," says Darren Peacock. "It was simply a matter of sink or swim for the pair of us.

"I was very aware of the fact that Paul Parker and Alan McDonald were very popular players at Rangers. I knew the fans would be watching our every move while those two were recovering from their injuries.

"When I watched the World Cup from Italy, I didn't guess that I would be joining the same club as Paul Parker, who played so brilliantly in that tournament for England. It seemed a million miles away from my own club Hereford.

"But Paul wasn't the only star of the World Cup that I was to meet when I arrived at QPR. Not long before, they had signed goalkeeper Jan Stejskal from Sparta Prague. He had shown that he was one of the best 'keepers in the world with a series of magnificent performances for Czechoslovakia in Italy.

"Playing in front of Jan did bring with it one notable problem in our first few games — the language barrier. Communication between a 'keeper and his defenders is vital but at that early stage Jan's English was non-existent.

"I'm sure that was the main reason why he had such a shaky start in the Football League. If it took a bit of getting used to for me to move from Division Four to Division One, you can imagine how difficult it was for Jan switching from the Czech to the English League.

"Slowly but surely Jan learnt some basic English that he would need in match situations. With that his confidence grew. He was soon proving his ability at crosses, as well as confirming what we already knew — that he is one of the world's top shot-stoppers."

The other main problem for Peacock and his new partner Andy Tillson was getting used to a completely new system of play.

"Before we joined QPR, Darren and I had been playing in a flat back-four in the lower divisions," explains Tillson. "But Don Howe, the manager who signed us for the club, wanted us to play as part of his well-established sweeper system.

"As Paul Parker had been the sweeper before his injury there had to be a replacement — and Don Howe picked me.

"That was quite a shock. I'd hardly ever taken on that role at Grimsby but now I was being asked to stand-in for one of the best around in the position.

"Playing at sweeper didn't get any easier over the next few months. I was having to play in a way totally different from what I was used to.

"At Grimsby, as a centre-back I always attacked the ball in the air. Now I had to resist that temptation. My job was to cover for the other two centre-backs, not to try to win all the balls in the air myself. It wasn't easy to break with my old habits.

"It might have been better if Paul had been around to give me some expert advice on the position. Unfortunately, his recovery programme meant he had to train separately from the rest of the squad so we had only the odd chance to talk.

"In the circumstances it was quite amazing that the team did so well in my first few months with the club. The longer we went into the season, the more our relegation worries eased.

"Towards the end of the campaign we were playing so well we even beat Liverpool 3-1 at Anfield. That would be a highlight of any season but was especially sweet for me in my first year in Division One.

"But we were knocked down a peg or two a couple of weeks later when we were beaten by champions-to-be Arsenal. That showed me I still had plenty to learn about life at the top."

Darren Peacock ended his first season at QPR showing his versatility as an emergency striker. But it was as a defender that he proved wrong those who said the only way he would make an impression in the game was by the length of his hair — which usually hangs well below his shoulders!

"Yes, people have always said that my hair would get me noticed more than any skill I might have on the pitch," says Darren. "I just hope I can keep proving that's not the case.

DEEP END!

ark Rangers' new boys
ANDY TILLSON and
DARREN PEACOCK

DARREN PEACOCK

"I suppose when I first came to QPR, the length of my hair was a good way of being noticed by the fans. On the other hand, if I made a big mistake, I might not want to be noticed!

"I'm always being told to get my hair cut. So every six weeks I go for a trim — but very little actually comes off! My attitude is that as long as I'm doing a good job, the manager won't bother about my hair.

"What he's concerned with is how I cope with First Division defenders — not how I look. That was a challenge I cherished right from the start at QPR.

"Fourth Division forwards aren't very subtle in their approach, but they can still cause you plenty of problems. A First Division striker thinks and acts a bit quicker than his lower division colleagues.

"I soon realised I had to be on my toes right from the start if I was to prove equal to the task. If I failed, I'd probably be back in Division Four before too long.

"The pressure is much greater in the top flight and Andy Tillson and I had to adjust to that fact very quickly. Mistakes were more likely to be punished if we weren't up to the job.

"But I don't think we did too badly between the two of us. By the end of the season we'd proved that two players from the Third and Fourth Divisions could take over from two top international players without the team collapsing around us," Darren points out.

124

YOUR PICTURE INDEX
COLOUR ● PIN-UPS ● ACTION

Printed and Published in Great Britain by D. C. THOMSON & CO., LTD., 185 Fleet Street, London EC4A 2HS.
© D. C. THOMSON & CO., LTD., 1991.

ISBN 0-85116-514-1

TOUGH

Liverpool's **JAN MOLBY** (left) competes with Everton striker **GRAEME SHARP** in a bid for vital possession.